# Work Like
# a Monk

# Work Like a Monk

## A Buddhist Guide to Embracing What Matters

## Shoukei Matsumoto

**TARCHER**
an imprint of Penguin Random House
New York

Tarcher
an imprint of Penguin Random House LLC
1745 Broadway, New York, NY 10019
penguinrandomhouse.com

Most Tarcher books are available at a discount when purchased in quantity
for sales promotions or corporate use. Special editions, which include
personalized covers, excerpts, and corporate imprints, can be created when
purchased in large quantities. For more information, please e-mail
specialmarkets@penguinrandomhouse.com. Your local bookstore can also
assist with discounted bulk purchases using the Penguin Random House
corporate Business-to-Business program. For assistance in locating a
participating retailer, e-mail B2B@penguinrandomhouse.com.

Book design by Shannon Nicole Plunkett

Hardcover ISBN: 9798217179657
Ebook ISBN: 9798217179664

Printed in the United States of America
1st Printing

The authorized representative in the EU for product safety and compliance is
Penguin Random House Ireland, Morrison Chambers, 32 Nassau Street,
Dublin D02 YH68, Ireland, https://eu-contact.penguin.ie.

# Contents

# Introduction

*S*wish, swish. A bamboo broom sweeps across the street, making a gentle, refreshing sound.

From the temple's main hall, you can hear the steady chanting of *sutras*.

As you walk through the temple cemetery, the scent of incense seems to carry the voices of those who have passed on, as if they are speaking to us even now.

In the temple courtyard, sparrows chirp, blending with the easy conversation of visitors. This place is filled with many sounds and voices.

Here, in these ordinary daily moments, lies what I call People's Buddhism—an approach to Buddhism that is woven into everyday life. I have practiced People's Buddhism for more than half of my life.

At the heart of People's Buddhism is what is known as *mindful listening*. Have you ever felt joy while sweeping up fallen leaves, noticing the gentle rustle of birds or the whisper of the wind? Or have you ever sat quietly, perhaps in meditation, listening to the soft voice within yourself? Maybe you've spent quiet moments in a church or a temple, feeling the presence of gods, Buddhas, or ancestors, as if they were speaking just beyond the silence.

Being fully present and open to these subtle voices in the here and now is the attitude we cherish as People's Buddhists.

In today's world, both at home and at work, we talk a lot about communication. Usually, when we think about communication, we focus on how to express our thoughts to others. But true communication is not just about relaying a message; it's about connecting. This means listening carefully not only to the words used, but also to the person behind those words. If more people practiced mindful listening, our shared life would feel richer and the world would likely become more peaceful.

Work has become a central part of our lives. In my work as an executive mentor, I have listened to many voices, from young employees in consulting firms, to factory workers, to global executives giving speeches. I have heard from people of all backgrounds, ages, and walks of life. I believe a monk's role is like that of a translator—not just translating between languages like Japanese and English, but also interpreting the Buddha's words for modern times, bridging different perspectives.

This book is written as a dialogue, with two people exchanging words and listening deeply. The Buddhist understanding I have gained over many years, as well as the insights I have learned from the working people I have met, are reflected in these two characters. While it may look like a story, every part is drawn from lived experiences and understandings I have gathered through real-life encounters.

Now, please, open your heart and listen to the conversation that awaits you.

# Character
# Description

### Businessperson (Narrator)

A man in his forties who often reflects deeply on the purpose of life. His grandfather was a temple priest, so he has felt a quiet closeness to Buddhism since childhood. He studied Western philosophy in college and entered the workforce at a time when jobs were limited. He joined a small, traditional company but soon struggled with the old-fashioned work style and left. Later, he earned an MBA and started his own human resources (HR) and organizational development firm with a data scientist friend. Their motto is "Making everyday work happier for people." Meeting with executives, HR managers, and employees, he constantly searches for what it truly means to create happiness at work.

## Temple Priest

A temple priest in his sixties who lives in a peaceful mountain temple. When he was young, he went through strict training as a monk. Today, he is known for his gentle smile and his warm welcome to all who visit. Though the temple is simple, it is well cared for, offering comfort and calm to people from the nearby community.

# Work Like
# a Monk

## Chapter 1

# People's Buddhism

## Life Noise

Look around the city, and you'll see many people wearing noise-canceling headphones. In a world this noisy, it's natural to want to shut it out and escape into your own space. It seems everyone is searching for "somewhere other than here."

Noise is not limited to sounds. In the morning, before I even get out of bed, my device overflows with news, messages, and updates. Scrolling through them while still half asleep, I let a stream of information flood my mind. We are living in a time filled with more information noise than ever before.

Would everything improve if we just turned off notifications? Not really. Silencing external noise or alerts doesn't silence the commotion inside us. If we pay attention, we realize how loud our inner chatter is—the endless stream of thoughts and desires: *I need this. I must do that. What do others think of me?* This inner noise, beyond our control, is the hardest kind to handle.

Perhaps this is why many people turn to mindfulness meditation, hoping for a brief moment of calm. Originally practiced as part of a Buddhist monk's training, meditation is now used by many as a noise-canceler—a way to bring calm into our over-filled inner world. Yet, for those of us immersed in daily life and work, without a serene temple to hand, shifting into a monk-like state of mind, even for ten minutes, is no simple task.

## What Is Happiness at Work?

I run an organization development company, supporting various companies in improving their organizational performance and well-being. My work includes bringing about organizational change, process improvement, talent development, and team building. My mission is "to make work-life happier for people."

But am I always happy with my own work? Not exactly. In today's business world, there's a trend toward measuring employees' well-being through various metrics, with phrases like *human capital management* or *well-being management*. Yet, do these approaches truly make workers happier? We try to measure people's abilities using fancy indicators, but every person is unique, and their condition can vary from moment to moment.

As human beings, we live in a web of relationships. When someone struggles with mental health issues, it is not a form of weakness, as it was once perceived, but is often a result of their past and present relationships placing them in difficult situations. The only way to understand this is by listening to them. Are we really listening to the genuine voices of our colleagues? I find myself asking this question every day.

I once had the chance to leave the city and travel to a rural area for work.

Looking out from the bullet train as it raced along at three hundred kilometers per hour, the scenery close to the tracks blurred like abstract art. Yet Mount Fuji, far in the distance, changed shape slowly, shifting to show different faces as we passed by. Living in a fast-paced city environment, it is easy to get caught up in the daily noise that surrounds us and lose sight of the bigger, slower picture—of what truly matters. To regain perspective, we need breathing room—time to slow down, leave space in our schedules, and refresh our minds.

After finishing my work that day, I strolled slowly

toward the station. On the way, I noticed a peaceful temple on a hillside and decided to stop in.

Passing through a mossy gate and crossing a small cemetery, I found an old wooden bench beside a pond. The temple grounds were a haven of nature; under a clear sky, I could hear birds singing against the backdrop of the mountain that rose behind the temple.

On a sign, a handwritten note said, "At 3:30 p.m., a *dharma* talk will be held in the main hall. All are welcome." It was now 3:40 p.m., so the talk had started ten minutes ago, but it would be a pleasant way to end my walk, so I decided to slip in nonetheless and listen to what the temple priest had to say.

Quietly sliding open the entrance to the hall, inside I saw folding chairs set out in two rows of three. An older woman in casual clothes—maybe a local out for a walk—and a pair of backpackers who looked like tourists were seated in the back row, facing the temple priest, who sat on another folding chair, with a life-size Buddha statue behind him. The only empty seats were in the front row. Feeling slightly self-conscious, I sat down and tried to focus on the priest's words.

*"People often ask, 'Why can't others understand me?' But since we each live lives shaped by different circumstances, it's natural that we don't fully understand one another. Each of us sees the world*

*differently, and that's our starting point. Because we can't understand each other easily, trying to meet halfway is what matters. Everyone thinks differently, and even parents and their children don't fully grasp one another's inner world. When we, imperfect humans that we are, find a moment of connection, of feeling understood, that's truly wonderful. It's worth celebrating."*

With that, the temple priest finished his talk.

## Listening First

Just as I stood up to leave, the temple priest caught my eye.

*"Welcome, and thank you for visiting. I am the head priest of this temple. If you have any questions, please feel free to ask."*

I was a bit taken aback by this direct invitation to ask questions. I had always pictured a monk's sermon as a long, one-way lecture, so this open, interactive approach surprised me.

*"I have talked by myself for long enough. The teachings of Gautama Buddha often arose from people's questions.*

*"Indeed, while the Buddha gave many talks to guide people, his approach, sometimes called 'tailored* dharma,' *meant adapting the teaching to each listener's needs and conditions. Just as a doctor first listens to a patient and uses a stethoscope to hear and understand their body's signals, the Buddha, known as the Great Physician, also began by listening. He would listen before he spoke."*

Even today, in business, we talk about the importance of listening.

*"However, there is much we don't know about what the Buddha's teaching sounded like, twenty-five hundred years ago. What language, what words, did he use to address people from so many different backgrounds? Without microphones, how did he make himself heard by thousands?"*

That is a mystery indeed.

*"There's a fascinating idea called the One Sound Doctrine. In the* Vimalakirti Sutra, *it is said, 'The Buddha spoke in one sound, and each person understood it in their own way.'"*

In my work as a corporate coach, I've seen how the same message can be understood differently by each person, depending on their mindset and situation.

*"One way to explain this One Sound Doctrine is that the Buddha may have repeated the same content over and over."*

Because people's understanding and growth depend on their own state of mind, the same repeated teaching could act like a "tailored *dharma*" for each individual. A message can resonate differently with an individual at different times.

*"Another, more daring interpretation suggests that the Buddha may not have spoken ordinary language at all. Instead, he might have continuously chanted the sacred sound 'om' ('aum')."*

This is an intriguing thought. Imagine that, instead of using everyday language, the Buddha conveyed his message through a single sacred sound. Each listener would then interpret this pure sound based on their own nature and circumstances. Without being limited by words, the sound itself would become the teaching, allowing anyone to receive it, regardless of the language they speak.

*"The Buddha's teachings have been passed down as countless* sutras. *Many begin with the phrase 'Thus have I heard,' and some* sutras *even seem to contradict each other."*

This could mean that the Buddha tailored his teachings to each listener, or that people heard the same message differently and shaped it into diverse teachings. The idea that the world is shaped by the observer's perception connects with certain Western philosophical ideas as well.

*"Without modern technology, Buddha's disciples turned his spoken teachings into written texts. When we monks chant these* sutras *today, we are trying to revive the Buddha's original voice."*

In the past, when I heard *sutras* chanted at funerals, I wondered why they were all in Classical Chinese—a language I, and many others, cannot understand. But if the essence lies in their sound rather than their literal meaning, my perspective on this changes. I had seen the words as a barrier, instead of a conduit through which to listen to the sound.

*"In Buddhism, direct oral transmission from teacher to student has always mattered because some things cannot be captured by written words*

*alone. Humans cannot live alone; we are rela-*
*tional beings, a concept we call* interbeing. *Bud-*
*dhism teaches us wisdom on how to live together*
*with others, even when we cannot fully under-*
*stand them. Practicing Buddhism is not some-*
*thing done in isolation in the mountains. It always*
*involves living companions."*


## Mindful Listening

*"Our temple follows the Nen Buddhist path.*
  *"And what is Nen Buddhism, you ask?*
  *"At its heart lies the practice of 'mindful lis-*
*tening.' This does not mean just using our ears;*
*it's about leaning in with our hearts and giving*
*our full attention to the person in front of us and*
*to the moment itself. It means having an open,*
*understanding attitude that lets us sense the Bud-*
*dha's voice and the voices of others. Through this,*
*we discover our own true voice as well.*
  *"I would sum up the spirit of Nen Buddhism*
*like this: 'Listen mindfully, then the voice will be*
*heard.'*
  *"The character '念' (Nen) is formed from*
*parts meaning 'now' and 'heart.' By speaking*
*and listening fully in this present moment, we*
*guide our hearts toward the voice.*

*"Through mindful listening, we tune our hearts to the Buddha's voice. As we listen to our own voice and sense its direction, the voice of Buddha begins to be heard."*

Listening not just with the ears, but with the heart. In Japanese, there is a phrase, *listening to fragrance*, which encourages an opening up of the senses, beyond their physical limitations. The English word *scent* comes from the Latin *sentio*, meaning "I feel." This means that, whether smelling or listening, you need to concentrate your attention toward the object with all of your five senses.

*"Traditionally, Japanese culture has encouraged an openness that doesn't divide perception into separate senses. People took in everything as a whole, not isolating sight, hearing, or smell. That's why, when we say Buddha listened, it goes beyond just our physical senses."*

To lean in and feel the "here and now" means to watch, to listen, and to sense. In Japan, this way of receiving comes naturally. Gently observing, sensing emotions beyond words, understanding the mood without explicit explanation—these are all ways we stay present, focused on subtle shifts around us.

*"In Nen Buddhism, we sum up this attitude in the word* listening *(聞).*

*"In Buddhism, the path to awakening often involves three steps: listen, contemplate, and meditate. First, you listen quietly. Then, you reflect on what you've heard. Finally, you internalize these insights through practice.*

*"The first of the three steps is listening. By listening to the Buddha's voice and noticing how it resonates within you, you begin to hear the polyphony of 'interbeing'—the harmony created when all existence resonates together with an open heart. Once you truly listen, contemplation and meditation follow naturally. This is what we call mindful listening in Nen Buddhism."*

So, how does *mindful* listening differ from *active* listening?

*"Mindful listening is not just a technique; it's a way of being. While you are still listening closely to the words, you're not only picking up the content of what is said; you're also sensing the speaker's feelings, reading their facial expressions, feeling their energy, noticing pauses, and even listening to the silences you share. Mindful listening includes all of this."*

Listening to silence, to stillness. It reminds me of John Cage's piece "4'33"," a composition performed entirely in silence. Mindful listening is bringing that concept, the value of meaningful silence, into our everyday lives.

> "At first, this way of listening may feel tiring. But over time, you will realize that devoting yourself fully to listening means fully opening up to the world. Listening goes beyond personal intention. When you truly listen, you naturally begin to hear. Perhaps you will find that you grow into a vessel that can receive both explicit and implicit voices. And listening with a calm heart can also soften the inner noise bubbling within us."

Listen until you begin to hear. I always thought *listening* and *hearing* were the same, but the temple priest seems to distinguish between them carefully.

## Ambient Buddhism

A deep gong sounded from the temple bell. I looked over my shoulder and noticed that the people who had been sitting in the back row had gone. Now, it was just me and the temple priest. Including the Buddha statue, we were three. The light shining through the paper screens behind the Buddha had a reddish tint.

I closed my eyes softly and listened.

The rustle of leaves in the trees outside. The gentle trickle of a nearby stream. The rhythmic knock of a *shishi-odoshi* bamboo fountain. The hum of insects. The distant sound of a conch shell, blown by a mountain ascetic.

These sounds had been present all along, but I had not heard them.

It was like my favorite ambient music. Brian Eno, pioneer of ambient music and thinker, said it can be "as ignorable as it is interesting." *Ambient* means "the surrounding environment," so *ambient temperature* is the room temperature around us. Eno's *Music for Airports* was meant to blend into the environment at the airports, enhancing the atmosphere without demanding attention.

My eyes were still closed as the priest spoke again in a gentle, clear voice.

*"In Japan, nature has never been something separate from us. Long ago, we used the term* jinen *to refer to nature, meaning things as they naturally are. It suggests that nothing exists alone— everything is interconnected, an interbeing. The meaning of* jinen *is close to 'habitat' or 'umwelt.'*

*"In the philosophy of interbeing, we don't see ourselves as isolated individuals. We understand that we are fundamentally connected to other humans and also to the wider world. This sense of interbeing, shaped by our surroundings (habitat) and our daily ways of being (habits), forms part of daily life and is the essence of our People's Buddhism—to listen wholeheartedly to everything that makes up our everyday environment. And to be aware that I, too, am part of this ambience."*

When mindfulness isn't limited to set times or places, but becomes part of daily life, this is what we might call Ambient Buddhism. Everything connects. This means listening to what's not visible, looking toward sounds we can't quite hear, sensing beyond usual perception. It also means allowing the past and future to join with the present moment. I remember reading an article in which Brian Eno described this feeling as the "Long Now."

## The Finger Pointing at the Moon

*"Even if we try to listen to Buddha's voice, at first we will not understand what he is saying or what it means."*

Through the act of listening, maybe something

"Buddha-like" can seep into our daily lives. But at first it may feel like grasping at fleeting pieces of happiness, something near yet hard to hold.

> *"If you have only one puzzle piece from a complex image, you have no idea what it forms a part of. Two pieces, three pieces, still no clear picture. It's frustrating. But if you keep listening, keep gathering pieces, sooner or later they start to connect, and that moment feels joyful. As you continue listening, you begin to sense an outline of what the final picture might be, making the process itself enjoyable.*
>
> *"The Buddhist path is often compared to a finger pointing at the moon. The moon you seek cannot be grasped directly; you only have the finger as a guide. As you live mindfully and listen to the Buddha's voice, the puzzle's shape emerges and the moon's outline becomes clearer. At that point, the puzzle itself is no longer the focus. The puzzle pieces are like the finger pointing to the moon, revealing its shape in the empty spaces. We sense the moon appearing where once we saw only puzzle pieces."*

I didn't expect to hear Bruce Lee's famous line from *Enter the Dragon* here: "Don't think. Feel! It is like a finger pointing away to the moon. Don't concentrate on the finger, or you will miss all that heavenly glory." But it all connects. All paths, indeed, converge.

After the temple priest's *dharma* talk, I headed out of the temple and down the path, aware that I had received something beyond words.

## Chapter 2

# Temple Morning

### *Aisatsu!* "Hello!"

I returned to my busy work routine, but the memory of that mountain temple stayed with me. I could sense that there might be something there to help me find clarity, something that hinted at a way to guide me through my inner uncertainties. I felt a strong desire to learn more from the temple priest.

Not long after my visit, I received a plain white envelope from the temple. Inside was a simple schedule of upcoming activities, printed in black ink. One entry caught my eye: "Temple Morning Gathering," it read. "We will share a glimpse of temple life: chanting *sutras*, cleaning, having tea and conversation. All are welcome."

When unsure, I always choose to go.

On the day of the gathering, the morning air was clear and refreshing. About ten people were present—some seemed local, others looked like travelers—ranging widely in age, background, and personality. The priest began by greeting us all warmly. After chanting *sutras* in the main hall, we walked around the temple grounds and tidied up. Then we shared a simple tea break and talked. It was brief, relaxed, and open to anyone. In my work, which focuses on target audiences and efficiency, it felt refreshing to join such a diverse and loosely structured gathering.

When everyone else had left, I found the priest putting away the cushions in the now-empty hall. I approached him and asked, "Could we talk for a bit?"

We sat down together on a bench by the main hall's veranda.

"Thank you for coming today," the priest said.

*"This isn't really an event in the usual sense. It's simply a way for me to share a part of my daily life as the temple's priest. There's no special intention or purpose behind the chanting, the cleaning, or the tea. I'm not aiming to teach Buddhism directly. Each person finds their own meaning in coming here. I just create a place where anyone who feels drawn can join and share the morning together."*

A gathering without a fixed purpose. On the schedule, just two words had leaped out at me: *temple* and *morning*. That was all that was needed. As long as there is a place and a time, people can come together.

"It's nice to start the day with a lively aisatsu, or greeting," the priest continued.

> *"The Japanese word* aisatsu *comes from Zen Buddhism, originally from the term* ichiaiissatsu, *which described how Zen masters and students would 'test' each other's understanding. The characters* ai *and* satsu *both mean 'to approach' or 'press forward.' In this way, greeting is about approaching each other's hearts and minds."*

I never imagined that a simple greeting could have such depth. Yet, on reflection, I saw that it is often true—many greetings are a bit mysterious. Since ancient times, people have greeted each other every day, using words that carry no new information. Even in our modern world that is so focused on efficiency, no one would ever claim that greetings were unnecessary.

There must be a primal, instinctual need that drives the widespread practice of greetings among living beings. The fact that greetings are ubiquitous, stretching across the world and back through history, suggests they carry a shared wisdom rooted in life itself.

*"Greetings appear everywhere, across cultures, beyond language or ethnicity. They take many forms: words, bows, handshakes, hugs, eye contact. Even animals greet each other in their own ways, maybe by touching noses or tails, or making certain gestures. Through greeting, we acknowledge the start of our shared time together."*

When we greet, we acknowledge and tune in to each other's presence. Through the sound of a voice, a facial expression, or a gesture, we sense each other in this exact moment.

*"When we say 'Good morning' every day, we begin to notice small changes in each other. Just as we look at the morning sky to guess the weather, a greeting lets us feel each other's mood and condition. All creatures, whenever they meet or part, acknowledge the here and now, sensing each other's state and offering the care that is needed in that moment."*

In my therapy studies, I learned that care can be communicated through a simple look, without a word or touch. Any form of communication— whether words, touch, a glance, or a simple gesture— can confer care.

## *Itadakimasu*

Is there such a thing as a "good" greeting?

*"A greeting allows us to recognize each other's presence and check on one another. Whether it's through a spoken word, a bow, or a handshake, we acknowledge the other person's existence.*

*"The Buddha taught us that to live well, we need to align our body, speech, and mind. When you greet someone, there's no need to force cheerfulness if that is not how you're feeling. Just greet naturally, as you are. Aligning body, speech, and mind begins with listening to your own voice first.*

*"It's also important to value the range of people you can directly share greetings with. By listening to each other's voices, we affirm our shared presence in this moment."*

Reflecting on my workdays, I realized that sometimes I go an entire day without saying "Good morning" aloud to anyone, especially when working remotely. Social media keeps us connected to countless people, but how often do we truly say hello in a meaningful way? Follower counts might suggest connection, but do those numbers reflect real relationships?

Research by anthropologist Robin Dunbar suggests that humans can maintain stable relationships with only about one hundred to one hundred fifty people, a limit shaped by our brain's cognitive capacity and observed in primates as well. Of those, perhaps ten or twenty are people we greet daily, perhaps even fewer in today's post-COVID world.

In Japan, everyday greetings mark moments of departure and return. When leaving, we say *"Ittekimasu,"* meaning "I'm going, and I'll come back." Those who remain reply with *"Itterasshai,"* which means "Go and return safely." Upon returning home, we say *"Tadaima"* ("I'm back"), and the reply is *"Okaeri"* ("Welcome back").

> *"At the temple, I greet people with the spirit of 'welcome home.' A temple is a place where anyone can return and say, 'Buddha, I'm home.' This home is open to all—not only to people, or to those alive today, but also to animals, plants, ancestors, and even future generations."*

I now see that when the temple priest said *itterasshai* at the end of the Temple Morning Gathering, it was an invitation to come and go freely.

> *"Our meetings and partings happen every day. In Japanese, we call this* ichi-go ichi-e, *which means*

*'a once-in-a-lifetime encounter.' Every encounter and parting is unique; a onetime event. Even with people we meet daily, wouldn't it be wonderful to treat each connection as if it were our last?"*

This same attitude applies to the Japanese custom of joining hands before and after meals; saying *itadakimasu* and *gochisosama* means that we appreciate every meal as a unique opportunity for gratitude.

*"Through meals, we receive the world's blessings, which become a part of us. The food we eat gives our bodies energy, which in turn we use to act and partake in the world. Before eating, we pause, hands joined, to recognize this connection. Each dish represents the life that was offered to create the food and the effort of everyone involved in bringing it to our table. By saying* itadakimasu, *we express gratitude for all these links in the chain."*

Eating sustains life, but it also connects us to the wider world. Each meal ties us to every being and bond that helped bring it to us. When we put our hands together in gratitude, we acknowledge and honor these connections, thanking each life and every effort that sustains us.

*"It's not just humans who greet each other. In Buddhism, we often say 'sentient beings' to refer to all forms of life. Imagine how wonderful it would feel if we recognized and greeted all living things we encounter."*

In Western philosophy, I learned that the word *sentient* comes from Latin roots meaning "to feel" or "to perceive." It shares its origin with words like *sentiment* and *sense*, suggesting that to be sentient is to be able to truly listen and feel.

*"We were animals before we were human. In the earliest days, long before we had language, we communicated much like other animals—through sounds and tones rather than words. Even today, we often voice emotions and feelings without choosing specific words. These vocal waves carry raw energy, feelings expressed through breath and sound, beyond language."*

As language developed, humans gained the power to think in complex ways. Civilization flourished and much was gained, but we also shifted our focus toward expressing thoughts through words, often ignoring the basic vibrations of life itself. Now that we try to handle everything as "information," we risk forgetting the significance of the voice as a direct expression of our being.

At its heart, a greeting is the exchange of voices.

## True Person

Everything in existence vibrates. The German physicist Max Planck once said that all matter exists only by virtue of vibration. In this sense, we are all resonant waves. Even if our ears cannot catch every sound, we still respond to vibrations, many of which lie outside our range of hearing.

The temple priest reached for a book on a nearby shelf.

*"A Zen teacher, Yamada Mumon, once taught that although our flesh-and-blood bodies are fragile and imperfect, within them resides a 'True Person without rank'—the pure human essence (Buddha-nature) that transcends social status, gender, age, wealth, or poverty. The noise of our everyday world often distracts us, so we rarely notice these inner waves that resonate in each person. We lose sight of them in others, but also within ourselves. These waves may be vast surges of energy or much quieter ripples. They may lie buried for so long that we almost forget they exist.*

*Yet these unspoken waves form the core of our True Person.*

*"We spend our lives dividing and sorting what we see, trying to fix the world into stable forms. In doing so, we overlook how everything keeps changing. When our mental noise settles down, we find a True Person who is always shifting, alive in each moment."*

I recall learning in Western philosophy that the word *person* comes from the Latin word meaning "to sound through" or "to resonate." In other words, a person is essentially one who bears a voice. Modern voice-authentication technology even treats each individual's voiceprint as unique—another reminder that each voice is distinct and personal.

*"A person's voice often reflects their energy, don't you think? But that energy changes with their environment. If we judge too much based on a single greeting, we risk missing important nuances. Buddhism teaches that 'all things are impermanent'; everything keeps changing, and nothing stays fixed forever."*

This is why I feel uneasy about fixed metrics in corporate HR surveys. Trying to measure the nature of dynamic, ever-changing human beings with static numbers seems limiting.

> *"The character for 'observe' in the name Kannon, the* bodhisattva *of compassion, literally means 'to observe sound.' In Buddhism,* bodhisattvas *are compassionate beings who stand between Buddha and humans, helping those who suffer. In the faith of Kannon, one of the most beloved and widely revered* bodhisattvas *in East Asia, every being emits some form of sound or vibration. Kannon hears these cries and extends a helping hand. The thousand arms of Kannon symbolize countless compassionate responses to those in need."*

I thought about how our bodies indicate to us that they are hungry by making a noise, or how skilled technicians in factories listen for changes in a machine's hum. A shift in sound signals a change in the system—human or mechanical. By listening rather than just looking, we pick up on subtle signals, noticing changes and patterns that might otherwise pass unnoticed.

## Buddha's Songs

During the Temple Morning Gathering, after we have greeted one another, everyone gathers in the main hall to chant *sutras*. These *sutras* are written in Classical Chinese, which I can't understand at all. I wondered if the monks, including the temple priest, were able to truly grasp the meaning of the words they chanted.

"Sutras *certainly have meaning. But I don't focus on the content while chanting. I focus on letting my entire body bring out the sound.*"

It struck me how different chanting is from simply reading aloud. I asked if it was about letting go of thinking and just being in the moment.

"*When I chant with full attention, my thoughts settle and I forget I'm even trying to think. My mind becomes very quiet, and I'm no longer thinking about the meaning of the words. Understanding them is a separate study.*"

I wondered aloud if it was at all like singing a song.

"*Yes, in a way.* Sutras *are like Buddha's songs, holding the Buddha's words and voice in written and spoken form. For nearly fifteen hundred years, Japanese Buddhism has kept these verses in their original Chinese rather than translating them.*"

*We value them more as sound than as everyday language."*

*Not grasping the meaning might help me chant more freely*, I thought—like listening to foreign songs without feeling the need to translate them.

*"When I chant, I pay attention to my own voice echoing in my body. The repetition makes it feel as if I'm becoming that sound; becoming the sutra, or the Buddha's words, or the Buddha's voice."*

I asked if each *sutra* has unique lyrics or melodies.

*"Different sects might emphasize certain sutras, but the vocal patterns share a lot in common. One key element is moving from the 'a' sound to the 'um' sound. Repeating that 'a'-to-'um' wave seems to fill the whole room around us."*

It reminded me of some yoga practices.

*"'A'-to-'um' is originally a sacred sound from India. Aligning with it is said to free us from ordinary cause-and-effect thinking. We begin life with an inhaled 'ah' cry, and we close it with a silent 'um.' Here in Japan, people often speak of the*

*'Ah–Um' breath. At many temple gates, you'll see two statues—one forming the 'ah' and the other the 'um'—symbolizing beginning and end together."*

## How Can We Become Good Ancestors?

In Japan, *sutras* are usually associated with funerals, although at this temple they're also recited on ordinary mornings.

For many Japanese, an encounter with Buddhism often begins with a family member's death, prompting reflection on their own mortality.

*"Our People's Buddhism includes memorial services called* hoyo. *Some are daily, monthly, or yearly. After a funeral, there's the seven-day service, the forty-ninth day, the first anniversary, then the third, seventh, thirteenth, and so on."*

Mindfulness focuses on the here and now, so I wondered how turning our hearts to those who have passed connects with that principle.

*"Traditional Japanese homes often have a* butsuma—*a dedicated room for a family altar, called a* butsudan. *This is a sacred space in the house, almost like a miniature temple."*

When I've visited older rural homes, I've often noticed these *butsuma* rooms with their family altars.

*"On the altar, alongside a Buddha statue, people usually place photos of ancestors or wooden memorial tablets called* ihai, *on which the deceased's posthumous name (*kaimyo) *is inscribed. We often say someone who has passed on 'becomes a Buddha.' Through these rituals, we honor both the Buddha and our ancestors."*

I'd heard that, in the past, many Japanese families offered morning and evening prayers at the family altar, reflecting on the Buddha.

*"Though it starts with remembering deceased relatives, it naturally expands into gratitude for other living beings and the land that sustains us. Over time, it leads to wishing for the well-being of the entire community."*

This suggests a widening sense of interconnectedness, from close family to a much larger web of interbeing.

*"In fact, most schools of Japanese Buddhism include a brief memorial verse in the daily* sutras *at home. Called* ekōmon, *this prayer expands the*

*merit of the chanting, not just for our own family or ancestors, but for all sentient beings. When we cherish someone close to us, it's a beautiful part of being human. At the same time, that closeness can create an invisible line that excludes others. The Buddha understood this duality in our attachments, seeing our love and concern alongside our need to widen our circle of care, holding both tenderness and sorrow together."*

We begin with those nearest to us and let that circle grow. It's an excellent design—even for leadership. Broadening our sense of how we interconnect helps true leadership flourish.

No matter the time or place, everyone has parents, who had parents, too. Whatever our background—our religion, culture, nationality, or gender—we all inherit from those who came before us, even if it's only our physical being.

*"The bond we have with our ancestors is both deeply personal and completely universal. It naturally becomes a meditation on life and death.*

*"This country has been struck by many earthquakes, tsunamis, and typhoons. These teach us how nature never fully yields to our will. Daily life sits side by side with extraordinary events,*

*and we live ever close to death. That's why we give thanks for simply being alive today.*

*"This practice not only honors our ancestors, but also reminds us that, one day, we, too, will join them. It's a ritual that reaffirms our mortality. Eventually, we, too, will become ancestors to people in the future. Standing at a family altar brings to mind not only the past but also the future—while letting us reflect on life and death right here in the present. It's about remembering those who have gone before us, looking toward those yet to be born, and asking ourselves, 'How can I be a good ancestor?'"*

"But how *can* I become a good ancestor for future generations," I ask the priest. It seems like such a big question, I feel overwhelmed at the prospect, and perhaps inadequate.

*"You don't need to leave behind some grand legacy. Think of all the unnamed people whose efforts, large or small, shaped the conveniences and technologies we enjoy right now. Everything around us is a gift from them."*

Hearing this, I felt maybe I, too, could contribute something to the future, even if only in small ways.

"I will begin by offering a kind word to someone in need each day, even if it's just a simple greeting," I said.

> *"Exactly. And sometimes we fail, but even failures can teach important lessons to those who come after us. That thought alone can give us courage, don't you think?"*

It reminded me of what Steve Jobs said in his Stanford commencement speech, where each morning he asked, "If today were the last day of my life, would I want to do what I'm about to do today?" By bringing that idea of "life's final day" into his morning, he reset his focus and renewed his determination.

By regaining what is known as the Long Now—a wider sense of time beyond just the present, a concept popularized by Brian Eno through the Long Now Foundation—we can feel renewed, as if each day is a fresh canvas for new ideas, creativity, and innovation.

## Walking and Pilgrimage

During the Temple Morning Gathering, after chanting in the main hall, we went outside to clean. As we walked around the temple grounds, surrounded by nature, I could hear leaves rustling, birds chirping, and the gentle flow of a nearby stream. Even my own footsteps felt different, adjusting to the ground beneath me.

> *"Walking, as a habit within our habitat, opens our awareness. It's as though my sense of self as a fixed inhabitant dissolves, releasing me from this shell of skin."*

I recalled how many philosophers were known to be enthusiastic walkers. Perhaps it's because walking provides the mental space for new ideas to emerge. Our brains even have a "default mode network," interconnected regions of the brain that typically activate when we daydream, but also often when we walk, and that help us organize our thoughts and reflect.

> *"Our ancestors, over millions of years, gradually stood upright and learned to walk on two legs. Unlike driving from point to point in a hurry, walking brings us back to a rhythm closer to our true nature. It reintroduces a calmer flow of time.*
>
> *"The simple act of walking can even become spiritual when done as a pilgrimage. Japan has an old tradition of pilgrimage, like the eighty-eight temple route in Shikoku."*

In Wakayama, the Kumano Kodō pilgrimage draws people from around the globe, much like the Camino de Santiago in Spain. The universality of pilgrimage across religions and cultures speaks to a shared human spirituality that is closely bound up with walking.

*"The intriguing thing about pilgrimage is that, although it seems directed at a goal, in reality it is the journey itself that matters most. Each stop is like a knot on a string, rather than a true endpoint. There is no ultimate goal."*

That felt unsettling to me, someone always chasing the next goal. "If there's no clear destination," I wondered, "what's the point?"

*"But, think: life itself is a journey. We all share the same final destination in 'death,' don't we? Therefore, true value lies not in hurrying, but in savoring each step of the journey."*

Maybe there's value in slowing down and walking at an easier pace. My daily life is so often consumed by chasing one goal after another. Even in today's world, where there is much talk of a "hundred-year life," I still feel rushed and my vision often narrows.

*"That's why we walk. When we walk quietly, we start hearing voices that we would otherwise miss. We are never truly alone in our steps. Even by ourselves, every stride connects us to countless moments across time and space. You can sense this not only in a mountain temple but also in the midst of a busy city."*

Psychologists sometimes talk about *awe*—the emotion of realizing we're part of something bigger than ourselves. It opens the mind, offers perspective, and is sometimes called the "small-self effect." Perhaps the simple act of walking holds that same hidden power.

## Cleaning as Mindfulness

I was probably in elementary school when I last swept fallen leaves with a bamboo broom. In Japan, from elementary through middle school, everyone cleans together daily, which I've always thought is a good practice.

*"Japanese people traditionally attach gratitude to cleaning. On one level, it's removing kegare, as in dirt, but on another, it's replenishing kegare, as in low energy. It's about truly paying attention and caring for both others and ourselves."*

I recalled how the connection between Japanese people and cleaning has, on occasion, been highlighted worldwide. In once such incident, after a World Cup football match, Japanese fans were shown cleaning the stadium seats on their own initiative. It was explained to the watching global community as "Japanese good manners," but I would suggest that they weren't doing it just to show politeness. Rather, it was like a greeting, an expression of gratitude for having been there, sharing the moment with everyone.

*"Cleaning is also a way to connect with a place. When you clean a space, this habit of care makes it sacred to you, shaping you as its inhabitant. For those fans who cleaned the stadium, that spot will always hold special meaning. By tending carefully to our surroundings, we build a bond with the space itself and, by extension, with each item we handle."*

I was struck by how well kept Japanese temples often are. Everything—rooms, wooden floors, old pillars—is kept neat and polished through daily effort.

*"In Japan's temples, cleaning has long been considered foundational practice. Simply sweeping fallen leaves and straightening up, beginning from*

*the nearest spot, is already a meaningful under-*
*taking."*

I realized that this, too, relates to the mindfulness
of being here and now.

*"Our surroundings connect us with who we are.*
*Messy surroundings can scatter our minds and*
*pull us away from the present. Grounding our-*
*selves in the here and now means bringing har-*
*mony both to us and to the space around us."*

Cleaning draws me back into the present moment
while also creating harmony with my environment.
Although I don't mind cleaning, my room sometimes piles up with clutter when I'm busy, and I
know many people struggle with it.

*"It's normal to think, 'Why bother? It'll just get*
*messy again.' But for us at the temple, cleaning*
*isn't simply a task to remove dirt or bring order*
*to a messy area. It's a daily habit that nurtures*
*our awareness of interbeing, just like chanting or*
*offering a greeting."*

Some feel more comfortable amid chaos. I asked
the priest whether we should aim for a certain
standard.

*"Existence simply is. Our minds are what label it good or bad. If someone finds peace in disorder, that's fine. 'Order' is personal. There's no final goal."*

Watching people cleaning around the temple, I noticed how refreshed and alive they all seemed.

*"It's a process you can enjoy creatively, not just a chore with a fixed endpoint. It fosters self-reliance—freedom in its literal sense."*

I suggested that some might hire a cleaning service or use a robot vacuum, and questioned whether there is anything wrong with relying on someone or something else.

*"Nothing at all. Temples sometimes ask parishioners to help or even use a cleaning robot. We live in a network of connections. Work, child-raising, or caregiving can leave little time, and our bodies don't always cooperate. Looking after our environment together can be a joint endeavor, drawing on one another's help as needed."*

So, even temples can have cleaning robots!

*"What matters is that practice differs from mere duty. No one else can meditate on your behalf; no one else can experience 'here and now' for you."*

The same way no one else can live my life for me, I suppose.

*"Even small acts count—straightening your desk or cleaning dishes. Everyday routines, like cleaning, are all forms of* samu—*mindful work that aligns you and your surroundings at the same time."*

Which explains why the temple priest always wears simple *samu* robes, ones that are for everyday routines as opposed to special rituals.

## Anything Can Be Practice

*"Here's a story for you. When Zen Master Dōgen went to China, he met a respected temple cook (the* Tenzo) *responsible for preparing meals for the monks. Dōgen asked, 'Aren't you too senior for kitchen duty? Couldn't you let someone else take over, so we can talk?' The monk answered, 'You, foreign visitor, have yet to grasp the essence*

*of the Buddha's way or the true meaning of words.'"*

What was the temple cook trying to convey?

*"In our* samu, *our temple work, what matters is giving complete attention to each task, letting awareness fill every corner. That kind of attentiveness helps us hear our own voices and the voices of others. It keeps us from getting carried off by the stream of thoughts and desires. I believe that's what the* Tenzo *was trying to show Master Dōgen."*

Thanks to the *Tenzo*, Dōgen was awakened.

*"Many people see daily household tasks as trivial compared to meditating or studying sacred texts. But even cooking demands full awareness of what's happening: how the ingredients look, how the heat or water is adjusted, what our hands are doing, and the state of our own mind. If our thoughts wander, we miss moments that never come again."*

It reminded me that mindfulness needn't be limited to special practices like seated meditation. Even household chores can be a form of practice, I observe aloud.

*"Anything in daily life can be practice, depending on how we approach it. Each movement, done with mindful attention, becomes a way to cultivate awareness. Our physical and mental conditions shift constantly—so does the world around us. The key is to quietly listen to each moment as it arises."*

We spend most of our day on autopilot. When we walk, we don't usually think, *Right foot, left foot.* Familiar tasks just happen, without conscious effort.

*"There's even a meditation focused on walking. Our daily routines run on habits, which are unconscious tendencies formed by past processes and backgrounds. Buddhism calls this* karma. *To know ourselves, we need to recognize these tendencies. Becoming aware of our ingrained habits—how we move, speak, and think—is one of the insights that mindfulness can provide."*

It would be wonderful if the chores we often dread could become something we look forward to. But shifting your mindset so drastically isn't easy.

*"Before starting a task, create a little ritual. Monks, for instance, put on* samu *robes before working. You might wear an apron or special clothes for cleaning, or open the windows wide to let in a breeze. It's a simple way to say, 'Okay, let's begin.'"*

I ask whether, once we start, we should try to focus fully.

*"It's fine if you can't. But often, once you begin, your mind naturally settles. It's not about having 'no mind' right from the start; you might arrive at this point gradually. Some days, you'll be too distracted—and that's normal. Just admit, 'I couldn't really focus today,' and move on."*

So concentration isn't forced; it develops on its own.

*"When you persist at your task in a mindful way, you will sense your physical space growing. You start to feel one with what you're doing. The area you clean becomes a place you feel connected to, and your body feels more and more like home. Your sense of space increases, and your capacity expands. It's an ever-widening awareness of your interbeing in this world."*

## Cleaning and Humility

If cleaning is a practice without a clear endpoint, what exactly are we aiming for? If we're just moving leaves from one spot to another, what does it accomplish? Sometimes it feels like we're imposing human order on natural processes.

*"Long ago, whenever disasters or national crises arose, an imperial decree would instruct people to clean shrines and temples. People believed that calamities happened because the places of deities and Buddhas were in a state of disorder."*

I choose my words carefully. From a scientific angle, I say, the second law of thermodynamics explains that molecular motion tends toward increased disorder over time. Pour milk into coffee and leave it alone, and they eventually mix. Without care, objects decay, mess accumulates, and entropy increases. In our bodies, this could manifest as neglect, leading to tooth decay or infections. So, in a sense, doesn't cleaning fight against the natural progression of things?

*"You have a point. Cleaning is, by definition, artificial. Sometimes destructively so—pulling weeds, for example, is arguably violent toward*

*other life forms. But life itself is a pushback against entropy; we sustain flow and balance in our bodies and minds by breathing, eating, and renewing ourselves. That cycle of entropy and renewal is what it means to live, and when that balance is lost, death follows. In that sense, there is both positive and negative."*

So, even as entropy is always happening, life perpetuates these ongoing cycles that preserve order.

*"Exactly. And that's why cleaning teaches us humility. Our bodies and minds are woven into nature, and we exist by relying on countless other forms of life. Recognizing these gifts—accepting the richness that sustains us—goes beyond notions of positive or negative."*

I realize that cleaning isn't just about tidying up. But if it's something so profound, I wonder aloud, where should I even start?

*"Right at your feet. When clutter piles up, we can't see what's in front of us—both physically and in terms of our wider awareness. The more our minds are scattered, the more likely we are to miss what's important."*

There's a Japanese saying: "Darkness lies at the foot of the lighthouse," meaning that by focusing too much on the distance, we may fail to illuminate what's right at our feet.

Perhaps it's best to begin here, step by step.

## No Noise, No Life

As I continue to visit the mountain temple, I wonder if I am beginning to change.

*"Each person finds their own way of changing. Buddhism talks about two paths: sudden awakening and gradual awakening. Sudden awakening can feel like the instant a pebble, kicked up by a broom, hits bamboo with a resonant crack: realization in a flash. Gradual awakening unfolds over time, maybe after years of wandering and practicing the Buddha Way. One day, you simply notice that your perspective has quietly shifted."*

It's understandable that most of us want a sudden awakening—something immediate and obvious. That's why self-help books promise such quick results.

*"It's natural to desire a sudden awakening. We tend to seek quick, easy answers. In Buddhism, we often call that tendency 'attachment.'"*

So we get attached to the idea of "letting go of attachments" as fast as possible—a paradox indeed.

> *"There's a saying: 'Sudden awakening, gradual cultivation.' Even if that awakening moment does come in a sudden flash, we can't control its timing. Our job is just to keep preparing and practicing. And even once we are awakened, the work of cultivation still goes on."*

I picture a pipe collecting debris—habits, thoughts, and experiences clogging our minds. Through mindful practice, whether by sitting or listening, we gradually unclog the pipe. Then, in a sudden shift, everything clears and energy flows freely. Yet that isn't the end of the process—life continues, and we keep practicing, just as we must keep cleaning the pipe.

> *"Awakening might sound grand, but it can be as simple as a moment of awe, when you feel something greater than yourself. If you hunt for it, it slips away. All we can do is stay open, quietly waiting."*

Waiting can be tough for me, as I always tend to focus on the next big goal.

*"Why are we all in such a rush? When we get an unexpected pause, why not savor it instead of getting anxious? Embrace the waiting. Whatever is meant to arrive will come when it should. Trust that timing, and wait."*

Thinking about it, I realize I seldom wait. Instead, I often rely on snap judgments, binary labels like *success* or *failure*, and judge everything in those terms. That mindset, that need for instant understanding of a situation, leads straight back to attachment. When we rush to categorize and judge, we miss the nuanced nature of reality and remain trapped in our narrow perceptions.

*"I'm the same. I, too, struggled with impatience, but in a different way. Nowadays I respect daily habits, but I used to ignore them. I was always rushing toward what I thought was 'true enlightenment.' Though I liked to keep things tidy, I avoided greetings, manners, or formalities—I dismissed them as mere ethics, not real Buddhism. I was, well, a stubborn monk."*

So the temple priest had times like that, too.

*"That's where Buddhism's compassion shows. It offers easy ways in for people like me. Initially, I*

*saw Buddhism more as a philosophy, not a religion. It answered the big questions: where we come from, where we go, why we suffer, and how to remove suffering. It all made sense in my head, and I felt I understood life's essence. I believed if I grasped Buddhism intellectually, daily routines and ethics were secondary."*

I ask if he eventually experienced a sudden awakening.

*"Not quite. I felt I understood, but something was off. Studying Buddhist theory didn't actually bring me closer to becoming Buddha; my life still buzzed with noise. In truth, I'd only been pretending to understand. When I realized that, I found myself unexpectedly supported by the habits I had gradually adopted over time.*

*"It was the simple routines—chanting familiar sutras, sweeping every corner of the temple, greeting those close to me—that shaped me in a bodily, not just intellectually, way. These small, steady practices became my personal Buddha Way. My once head-heavy approach found physical balance, and I learned to live alongside life's inevitable noise."*

So maybe that failed attempt at sudden awakening led, over time, to a gradual awakening.

*"It's not necessarily a binary between 'sudden' or 'gradual.' Both describe the same process from different angles. In Zen, cleaning might be seen as polishing one's heart, removing dust. In Nen Buddhism, we might talk about noticing how the heart persists, dust and all. Either way, I'm still sweeping every day. There's always more dust, no matter what."*

I used to think Buddhism was just a way to cancel out the noise of life, a mindfulness technique to hush sounds, minimize data overload, and quiet the inner chatter. And while that is partly true, I see now that it also teaches something else: to accept the noise, even befriend it, until it is no longer noise.

No noise, no life.

Hearing it reminds me: the noise is here, and so am I, alive today.

## Chapter 3

# People's Buddhism at Work

Since that first time, I've been visiting the mountain temple almost every month for its Temple Morning Gathering. One year, for an annual memorial service, I even brought my partner and child along so we could all attend as a family.

Each time I went to the temple, I asked the priest for a few moments of conversation. In Buddhism, *kunju* is a term that refers to how one can absorb the essence of a teaching simply by being nearby—like catching a gentle fragrance in the air. I hadn't formally become a disciple, but I believed, as the old saying goes, that even an observer at the gate can still learn from the *sutras*. Just being in the temple's atmosphere, I thought, might allow its teachings to naturally permeate my mind.

The priest's words were always straightforward. In an era of increasing business complexity, his simplicity struck me as precisely what people need. As I continued my monthly visits, I felt driven to share the lessons I was receiving with those in the business world. I decided to begin a newsletter for my clients: managers, HR professionals, and employees I had come to know through coaching. These are some notes and reflections inspired by the temple priest, intended to resonate with our modern workplace environments.

## No Job in Life Is a Bullshit Job

David Graeber introduced the idea of modern "bullshit jobs" with the following observation:

*In the year 1930, John Maynard Keynes predicted that, by century's end, technology would have advanced sufficiently that countries like Great Britain or the United States would have achieved a 15-hour work week. There's every reason to believe he was right. In technological terms, we are quite capable of this. And yet it didn't happen. Instead, technology has been marshaled, if anything, to figure out ways to make us all work more. In order to achieve this, jobs have had to be created that are, effectively, pointless. Huge swathes of people, in Europe*

*and North America in particular, spend their entire*
*working lives performing tasks they secretly believe*
*do not really need to be performed. The moral and*
*spiritual damage that comes from this situation is*
*profound. It is a scar across our collective soul.*[*]

According to Graeber, our "collective soul" suffers from this hidden wound. We live in a time of overflowing goods and data; production doesn't cease, nor does consumption.

Why? Because our economic system can't function if the wheels of production and consumption ever come to a halt.

Caught in a loop of buying, consuming, and discarding, we sometimes sense that our very lives are treated as disposable. To numb this emptiness, we throw ourselves into more work, thereby fueling yet another round of perpetual production and consumption.

Yet there's a hopeful side to this story. In the broader scope of life, there is no such thing as a truly bullshit job. Everything we do to sustain our lives carries meaning. Therefore, we should pay closer attention to the subtle, easily overlooked acts that support our day-to-day activities at work and in wider life.

---

[*] David Graeber, *Bullshit Jobs: A Theory* (Simon & Schuster, 2019).

These seemingly small, everyday tasks and connections sustain and ground us; they offer a richness often absent from those duties that we "secretly believe do not really need to be performed." Especially now, when so much has shifted into the digital realm, we might discover that what genuinely nourishes our mental and physical well-being is rooted in hands-on, tangible experiences.

Whether at home or in professional settings, every corner of our daily routine contains something of real value, if only we care to notice.

## What Matters Is Returning, Not Just Maintaining

Life inevitably pulls us away from our ideal path now and then. We all face times when our response to external noise leaves us feeling helpless, aware that we "shouldn't" take this path, but unable to stop.

This is where the Buddhist tradition of *uposatha* comes in. Dating back to the time of the Buddha, *uposatha* was a dedicated moment for practitioners to pause and reflect—not in a single large gathering, as India was vast and contained thousands of monks, but in smaller groups based on geography. Twice a month, on the new moon and full moon, these groups would meet to study the Buddha's guidance on living mindfully, examine how well they had followed it, and admit where they had fallen short.

In a way, it worked like a decentralized network, a spiritual decentralized autonomous organization (DAO), enabling practitioners to support one another in maintaining a mindful life. This collective practice underpinned early mindfulness training. Living out these ideals isn't easy, and by gathering together, the practitioners helped one another stay on track.

The priest from the mountain temple taught me that the heart of *uposatha* is not maintaining, but returning. It's not a rigid assessment that penalizes failure; rather, it is a piece of wisdom that, if followed, encourages good results. There's no judgment in slipping up; the point is to restore ourselves for our own well-being.

Reflecting on this, I realized how true it is. Our habits shape who we are. Since childhood, each of us has unconsciously absorbed countless behaviors, words, and thoughts. Unhealthy lifestyles can develop from certain habits, yet healing also comes through positive lifestyle changes.

From personal experience, I know that good habits bring balance to mind and body and ultimately enrich life. Yet maintaining those habits is challenging. That is why we humans gather socially. By coming together, we renew our commitment and guide ourselves back to where we want to be.

## We Are Interbeing

A company is an organization, yet the original meaning of the word points to "companionship." Now more than ever, we need to reconnect with that core idea.

In Buddhism, a community united by purpose rather than by birth is called a *sangha*. The Buddha taught that nurturing good companions is not merely part of the path; it *is* the path. Our journey is never truly solitary; it is one we walk alongside others.

Why walk together instead of alone? During difficulties, companions help us stay upright. When we stray, mentors and peers can show us the way back. Still, in our adult, professional lives, we often insist on being "independent," as if needing support is a sign of weakness or something shameful.

Yet Buddhism sees us as fundamentally *interbeing*. This view is known as *interdependent co-arising*: all things come into being through a vast web of interlocking influences. In simple terms, who we are—the inhabitant—is constantly being shaped by where we are—our habitat—and what we do—our habits. Each moment, and each individual, is shaped by countless forces so that a shift in any one part ripples outward.

One Buddhist text illustrates this through the image of "Indra's net." Picture each node in a great cosmic web as a jewel, reflecting and illuminating every other jewel. Likewise, our own lives reflect and affect one another's. "I" exist only as a facet of this network, shining through mutual resonance.

In Japan, there's a cultural sense of companionship that can even extend beyond humans. Pilgrims, for example, wear garments bearing the phrase "Two Traveling Together," reminding them they journey with a spiritual guide. Someone meditating alone in a mountain retreat might still feel an affinity with animals, plants, and the natural world.

Suffering often arises not because we are physically alone, but because we shut ourselves off from the world. When used wisely, connections help us heal; when we isolate ourselves, even our strengths can become burdens. By staying open, we learn to embrace being alone with ourselves, which in turn allows us to feel comfortably connected with others who have also embraced genuine solitude.

So, in the deepest sense, can our workplaces truly be called *companies*—places of real companionship?

## Fellowness as a Moral Dimension

People's Buddhism encourages us to open our hearts. While mindfulness is often viewed as a solitary practice—sitting quietly, alone—the deeper aim is to move beyond the individual "me" and embrace the interconnected "we," allowing ourselves to connect with others.

A helpful framework here is Professor Yuichi Tei's concept of *moral dimensions*, originally developed to imbue artificial intelligence (AI) with moral thinking. It is grounded in the principle that "the scope of 'us' defines the scope of 'me.'"

**Fellowness Level 1:** An absolute, self-contained "I," recognizing no others.

**Fellowness Level 2:** Awareness of others arises, but the self is defined by comparing oneself with them.

**Fellowness Level 3:** A collective "we" emerges, such as a team, a company, or a nation. However, this includes distinctions between "inside" and "outside," potentially creating adversaries.

**Fellowness Level 4:** Transcends divisions, guided by compassion and a broader ideal of coexistence across artificial boundaries.

Although Tei's original theory stops at Level 4, Buddhism suggests an additional step:

**Fellowness Level 5:** Expands "us" beyond a limited sense of humanity to include nature, ecosystems, ancestors, and future generations, recognizing our shared "humanness" as one part of this larger web.

It's important not to see these levels as labels by which to judge or rank people. Rather, we need to understand that we each carry all of these levels within us. For instance, we may exhibit Level 1 behavior as an infant, when absorbed in an activity, then shift to Level 2 when forming likes and dislikes. We can reach Level 3 by contributing to our workplace or country, experience Level 4 by practicing empathy across different cultures or beliefs, and sense Level 5 in moments when we feel our smallness in the vast cycle of life.

However, Level 5 also raises complex questions, especially when we consider AI. If an AI were to adopt a fully holistic view of nature, it might see humanity as an obstacle and decide to remove us for the sake of the larger ecosystem—a dangerous possibility.

Nevertheless, modern trends like diversity, equity, and inclusion (DEI) and multi-stakeholder capitalism represent attempts—however limited—to move beyond a purely profit-driven paradigm. From a Buddhist perspective, however, any form of capitalism remains deeply tied to the concept of ownership, which is fundamentally at odds with the principle of detachment—that is, freedom from attachment or clinging.

From the viewpoint of interbeing, this planet is the habitat of all sentient beings, and we humans are merely one among many inhabitants. Just as property boundaries mean nothing to ants and national borders are irrelevant to birds, one might envision a world where all people can move freely and find their rightful place. Yet, in reality, a small number of individuals possess vast amounts of vacant property while many struggle without a home. Seen from space, this stark imbalance would seem absurd.

Despite this contradiction, contemporary economic models such as Kate Raworth's *doughnut economics* attempt to incorporate nonhuman entities into our economic frameworks. They align with Buddhism's concept of *interbeingness*, which recognizes every part of nature as a potential contributor to a collective awakening.

A deeper pursuit of this ideal reveals just how difficult it is to realize on a large scale. We must remain conscious of the fact that even the idea of *inclusion* reflects a lingering human-centered perspective—one that assumes humans have the authority to grant or deny participation to other beings. True alignment with the Buddhist principle of interbeing requires a deeper shift in how we perceive our relationship with the world.

We begin by acknowledging that we are imperfect. We often fall short of Level 5. Recognizing this is the starting point for true growth.

## Cleaning Connects People and Places

When individuals choose to clean their own workplace, they're doing more than just tidying up.

They are restoring the space to a state where everyone can work safely and efficiently. There's no single "right" way to do this. Each workplace has its own mix of people, roles, and habits, all of which change over time. Knowing how to keep things clean in a flexible, adaptive way is a key sign of leadership ability.

Cleaning also builds stronger teams. Whether at work or at home, we each occupy a physical space on this planet with the body we have. Therefore, cleaning the workplace first thing in the morning means making the shared environment ready for everyone to start the day together.

It's true that, on paper, employment is a contractual relationship: people trade their work for financial compensation. This can feel mechanical, like we are just cogs in a bigger machine. Larger companies often try to offset this with benefits and backup systems, but this can lead to treating people in ways that feel transactional and impersonal.

Yet no matter where we work, the present moment is always unique. Our minds and bodies are here, now, in this particular company. Just as birds ignore borders when they choose a branch to land on, this workplace has become our immediate habitat. Look around: you and your coworkers share this branch, an unlikely meeting place among countless possibilities in the world.

Cleaning with your colleagues each morning is a way of saying "We occupy this branch together, so let's care for it together." A true home is not something handed to us; it's something we create. By cleaning, we make the space truly our own.

Even dedicating just five minutes a day helps. Pick any method that works. By setting and maintaining a routine, you'll notice a more positive energy spreading through the workplace.

### A Way to Solve Problems without Solving Them

In Zen Buddhism, there is a practice known as *kōan*. It poses a riddle-like question from a master, something to ponder deeply rather than solve in the usual sense. The Korean Zen practice often asks, "What is this?" while the Hindu sage Ramana Maharshi in India emphasized, "Who am I?" Across many traditions, focusing on a single, unanswerable question has always held universal appeal.

Interestingly, *kōan* practice parallels certain business approaches, such as critical thinking and *un-learning*. In most corporate settings, employees are trained to solve problems within established frameworks, reflecting logical and scientific thought. But *kōans* push us beyond those boundaries. They challenge us to question our basic assumptions, inviting insights that arise outside familiar patterns. This aligns with the idea of unlearning—letting go of long-standing habits to adapt and innovate.

A *kōan* isn't about finding a final answer. It's about confronting the very act of questioning and, in the process, transforming ourselves. We're trained—almost programmed—to solve problems quickly, which is useful for logical tasks but can also trap us within rigid constraints.

*Kōans* can't be resolved by standard problem-solving. Instead, they require a shift to take place within the person who perceives the problem. Once that shift happens, the "problem" itself often dissolves.

Choices are another example of a prepackaged problem, where we have the illusion of autonomy but are in fact given discrete options: either *this* or *that*. Exposure to *kōans* helps loosen our grip on such constraints. In Studio Ghibli's *Spirited Away*, Chihiro's challenge is to identify her parents, who have been turned into pigs. The witch demands an either/or choice, but Chihiro breaks the spell by realizing, "They are not here." Faced with a *kōan*, she steps outside the given structure.

As we learn language, we build a maze of mental constructs as we go. A prelinguistic baby offered a choice of two items might grab both of them or ignore both of them. Buddhism offers a pathway for adults to free themselves from these limiting constructs—a process of unlearning that, instead of adding new rules, releases us from old ones.

Albert Einstein famously remarked, "A new type of thinking is essential if mankind is to survive and move toward higher levels." When we grow overly proud of our logical prowess or problem-solving skills, that might be the time to pause, look down, and notice the shadow our own mindset casts.

## Four Stages of Life

Kūya, a revered monk of the Nen Buddhist tradition, lived as a humble mendicant, staying close to ordinary people and embodying the spirit of People's Buddhism. Guided by deep compassion, he shared whatever offerings he received with the sick and the poor, showing a profound example of selfless service.

One day, a learned monk asked Kūya, "How should one live to find peace in the next life?" Kūya's answer was short yet impactful: "Only when you let go can you truly find freedom." With that, he departed.

This idea of "letting go" is deeply relevant to modern life. Many people believe that accumulating possessions or wealth leads to greater freedom. Yet, paradoxically, the more we acquire, the more we become tied down by it all, and genuine freedom slips further away. Real freedom isn't found in being bound to endless acquisition, but in having a mind free of burdens. For those strongly influenced by a wealth-centric mindset, purposeful reflection and conscious practice are essential to shift one's perspective and lifestyle.

A helpful framework for this comes from the Indian concept of the Four Stages of Life. The first stage is the student phase, devoted to learning; the second is the householder phase, centered on work and family; the third is the forest-dweller phase, stepping back from daily duties to reflect; and the final stage is that of the renunciant, preparing to face life's ultimate transition.

In our present era, where people commonly talk about living to one hundred, retirement at sixty-five no longer seems like an "end." Instead, it can become the start of something new. More individuals are launching businesses or pursuing second (or third) careers, repeating aspects of the householder phase multiple times. The tradition of embracing life's impermanence in later years is now being postponed. In older Buddhist teachings, the word *elder* (*roshi*) signified deep wisdom and maturity. Our modern challenge is not, in fact, an aging population, but the lack of true elders who exemplify that wisdom and move beyond mere material accumulation.

Given the many transitions in this extended-lifespan world, it's easy to feel overwhelmed. This is why I propose applying the Four Stages of Life as a structured approach: roughly twenty-five years as a student (up to about age twenty-five), twenty-five years as a householder (up to about age fifty), twenty-five years as a forest dweller (up to about age seventy-five), and then a renunciant phase thereafter.

Of course, plunging into a contemplative life the moment we turn fifty may feel daunting. Instead, we might want to mix and match different elements. At fifty, for example, we could adjust to a balance of 70 percent work, 20 percent learning, and 10 percent reflection. That way, we can gradually adapt to a new stage without clinging too tightly to what came before.

In moments of major life change, consider Kūya's teaching about "letting go." By putting it into practice, we ease ourselves into whatever stage awaits, maintaining the freedom to learn, grow, and discover anew.

## Releasing Perfection through
## Focus and Letting Go

Zen Master Dōgen once wrote, "To study the path of the Buddha is to study the self. To study the self is to forget the self. To forget the self is to be enlightened by all things. To be enlightened by all things is to cast off the body and mind of both self and others." In Zen, awakening is not a separate goal at the end of practice; rather, the practice itself is awakening. The journey and the destination are one.

Buddhism highlights the need to release perfectionism rather than chase it. Various teachings underscore this idea.

## The Path Has No Final Endpoint;
## It Is Infinite

Completion is considered around 80 to 90 percent, cautioning against the pursuit of absolute perfection.

One relevant term is *Myo-Kanzatsu-Chi* (妙観察智), often rendered as "Subtle Discerning Insight." This concept reminds us that overfocusing can narrow our perspective and cause us to miss what lies just beyond the immediate task. Take cleaning, for example. When we become overly focused on perfection, our scope narrows and we miss what lies just beyond the task at hand. True wisdom lies in knowing when to refine our focus and when to let it go, balancing close attention with the ability to step back.

This interplay between *focus* and *letting go* applies equally in business. Project planning often demands meticulous detail, but pausing periodically to step back and reassess can foster adaptability and deeper insight.

Across Buddhism, we're reminded that the path itself has no ultimate goal and that perfection is essentially an illusion. Sweeping fallen leaves in autumn serves as a daily reminder: the work is never finished, because more leaves fall as soon as we tidy up. In both mindfulness and business, neither constant intensity nor unbroken ease alone is sufficient; genuine progress comes from weaving together concentration with relaxation.

## Living the Middle Way

Buddhism teaches what it calls the *middle way*, urging us to find balance rather than gravitate toward extremes.

In practice, this means avoiding both unnecessary hardship and excessive indulgence. Take the example of Gautama Buddha, who left home at twenty-nine, spent six years in harsh asceticism, and attained awakening only when he turned away from such severity and chose a balanced path. In the workplace, we can see a similar principle: growth often arises from experiences that are neither too demanding nor too relaxed.

The phrase *middle way* might give the impression of indecision or mediocrity. I felt that way myself when I started visiting the mountain temple. I had been expecting sharp, challenging teachings rather than the gentle idea of a balanced path. But over time, as I took in more Buddhist perspectives and saw how they applied to the complexities of life, I began to see the importance of this approach.

*Extreme paths* can be direct and dramatic, seeming bold at first glance. Yet they can also serve as the easy way out, providing quick resolutions that fail to account for how often reality shifts. A single decision, however definitive it may feel, can quickly become misaligned when the situation changes.

In contrast, *walking the middle way* seems straightforward on the surface but is actually quite difficult in practice. If there were fixed start and end points, or clear boundaries, it would be easier to pick the center. But in a boundless universe, there's no single reference point for "the middle." Our everchanging, multifaceted world simply doesn't offer a permanent midpoint.

The same is also true in the workplace, where the

middle way will emerge only through repeated decision-making. A leader should strive to be thorough without pursuing perfection, and be flexible without being lax. This ongoing balance of diligence and recalibration is critical for sustained growth. Seasoned leaders know that successfully guiding a team often hinges on adapting to shifting demands with steady composure.

The middle way is an ongoing journey, a series of constant adjustments to find the "center" of who we are at any given moment. Like walking a tightrope, leaning too far in one direction will cause you to topple; overcorrect, and you will imbalance the other way. Success lies in a continuous process of fine-tuning, where leaders nimbly shift between firmness and flexibility to support their teams. This dynamic, evolving balance defines the essence of the middle way.

Ultimately, walking the middle way is a lifelong endeavor with no fixed endpoint, a perpetual quest to find our center.

## The Trap of Purpose

Dreams, intentions, purpose, goals—whatever we call them, everyone carries visions of who they want to be or what they wish to achieve. Desire, called *attachment* in Buddhist terms, can indeed fuel our vitality. Yet this force is delicate, and managing it can prove challenging.

The more determinedly we chase our dreams, the narrower our perspective may become. Fixating on "This is indispensable," or "It must succeed no matter what," can close off other avenues of possibility. Buddhism teaches that when desire stems from a need to control outcomes, it often breeds suffering. Releasing that tight grip allows for greater openness and flexibility.

Committing firmly to a goal has its power, but paradoxically, it can also highlight what remains absent. If an urgency or emptiness lingers despite high aspirations, step back and ask yourself, "Am I actually saying that I'm not enough—or that something is missing?"

Working toward significant goals is commendable. Whether or not we achieve them is part of life's interwoven tapestry; besides, success and failure are rarely absolute. A moment of failure, seen from a different angle or given time, may reveal or lead to an unexpected success. Purpose should act like a guiding star rather than an anchor, shaping our direction without weighing us down.

To find balance, avoid clutching your purpose too tightly. Instead, approach it from a calm distance, trusting that what matters most lies in what you can do right now. Regularly pause to reassess your goals, allowing the journey to remain adaptable. Value the meaning held in everyday life, where each experience informs the path ahead.

## What Makes a Good Conversation?

Many workplaces now schedule regular meetings between managers and their individual team members, setting aside time for one-on-one conversations and acknowledging the importance of this interaction. But what truly makes a conversation "good"?

In some ways, a conversation resembles shared meditation. It can't be reliably measured by scores or metrics. A fulfilling conversation often carries a sense of "completeness," a connection that goes beyond mere understanding or agreement and into a kind of shared presence.

Conversation also parallels music: you can practice an instrument to become proficient, but technical skill alone doesn't guarantee a moving performance.

When I was a child, I often visited a nearby well. To get the water flowing, you first had to pour in a little water. Only then would cold spring water begin to flow. I still remember the invigorating chill of that water on a hot summer afternoon.

Dialogue operates much like that well.

When two people sit down to talk, it's as if there

is a "well of words" between them, but it is initially silent. Then, one person offers a single word or remark—the priming water. If both participants continue to "pump," making an earnest effort to listen and respond, words eventually flow freely, no longer forced. At that point, the conversation becomes effortless.

Of course, priming the well and pumping do involve skill, which develops through practice. However, even the most skilled practitioner cannot control the source of the water itself. Sometimes the well is dry; sometimes external circumstances muddy the water. Whatever comes to the surface must be accepted and worked with. When dialogue is aimed less at obtaining the perfect "water" and more at open, genuine exchange, it unfolds naturally.

Professor Takashi Iba from Keio University, known for his work on autopoiesis, says that truly creative, timeless works go beyond their individual creators. They tap into a collective unconscious, a current of creativity that flows through all humanity. This deeper undercurrent has also been referred to as the *polyphony*.

Writers like Haruki Murakami and filmmakers like Hayao Miyazaki often note that they don't fully "create" their works; instead, the stories seem to emerge on their own, as if the characters are speaking or the events are unfolding of their own accord.

This process of *yielding to emergence* is vital in any creative endeavor.

In a business setting, consider brainstorming sessions. For instance, Pixar fosters an *unstructured ideation* process, where people share ideas freely, starting by putting thoughts out there, similar to priming a well. Without rigid agendas, ideas evolve organically, paving the way for genuine innovation.

For leaders, the takeaway is clear: strong dialogue begins with openness and trust. Creating a space where participants feel safe to share can allow insights and solutions to naturally appear, much like water rising from a well that has been properly primed.

## Expanding the Capacity for Emotions through Sorrow

In Buddhism, sorrow is not considered a negative emotion. Rather, the capacity to feel and share sorrow deeply, to experience your own pain and truly empathize with someone else's, is seen as a powerful strength.

Emotions can either contract or broaden our ability to connect. While anger or fear may isolate us, feelings of joy and sorrow can expand our understanding. When we engage with sorrow, we open ourselves to others, discovering an empathy that

goes beyond mere sympathy and transcends individual experiences. This *sorrowful empathy* helps us
experience life as a shared, interconnected reality.

Among all emotions, sorrow has a unique ability
to create space for others. Experiencing profound
sorrow can expand our emotional capacity, enabling
us to hold and honor the full scope of human experience: joy, anger, love, grief. Being open to this
emotional range helps us appreciate the complex,
sometimes contradictory tapestry of life.

Focusing solely on happiness or joy can be short-
sighted. Sorrow enriches our inner life, preparing
the ground for more vivid, varied emotional experiences and forging a deeper bond with the world
around us. In Buddhist thought, *sorrowful empathy*
is central to a compassion that extends to all living
beings, opening a path that connects both the human and the transcendent.

For true well-being, we must learn to hold both
joy and sorrow. When we see sorrow not as something negative but as a teacher that enlarges our
hearts, it changes not only how we approach our
daily ups and downs, but also how we view life itself.

## Conversation and Debate

In Buddhism, there is a concept called *mind only*,
which holds that everything we perceive of the

world is shaped by our minds. In other words, my view of the world differs from yours, and while the facts may be singular, the reality that each of us experiences is unique. Recognizing that genuine mutual understanding is inherently difficult helps us avoid the frustration that can arise when attempting to fully comprehend another person's perspective, and cautions us against trying to force our own version of reality onto someone else, which often leads to conflict.

Why, then, do we engage in conversation? Conversation is not about attaining total understanding, but about acknowledging and mourning our inability to do so. Out of this shared recognition of imperfection arises connection. By accepting and sharing our mutual incompleteness, we discover hope.

In today's corporate world, where diversity, equity, and inclusion are encouraged more than they were in the past, it is crucial to create a space where different views can coexist. Although debates can help teams make decisions and set strategies, they can also leave lingering unease, since the final outcome rarely reflects everyone's reality. Here, conversation becomes a process for addressing that collective discomfort and building empathy and unity.

Imagine a team-building exercise where colleagues discuss not just immediate problems and solutions but also their varied perspectives. Just as casual social conversations can help foster trust, authentic conversations in the workplace can lead to deeper connections and resilience.

Leaders can organize "listening circles" before major discussions, inviting team members to share thoughts without interruption or criticism. Such an inclusive setting helps each person feel heard, enhancing the quality of collaboration when formal debates begin.

Debate and dialogue serve different purposes. Conversation should come first—establishing bonds and understanding—and also take place afterward, soothing any wounds that may arise from the intervening debate. Often, it only requires a few words: simply sharing the same space, listening to the silence, and attending to one another can be enough.

Even if perfect understanding remains out of reach, engaging in meaningful conversations about our differences is still worthwhile. We share a common habitat, interlinked by our very existence, and dialogue is one way to strengthen those links.

## How Buddhism Views Solitude

What does Buddhism say about solitude?

The scriptures offer a memorable phrase, "Born alone, die alone, come alone, go alone," suggesting that, at our core, we live as solitary beings; none of us can fully replace or merge with another. Yet rather than breeding isolation, this reality can actually foster deeper empathy. When two people understand the profound nature of their solitary existence, they can connect in a more honest way, with a shared recognition of what separates them.

Buddhist practitioner Stephen Batchelor refers to this as "solitude," underscoring how suffering stems not from being alone but from shutting ourselves off from the world. By remaining open to the world, we discover the capacity to embrace solitude wholeheartedly. Here lies a form of spirituality grounded not in the supernatural but in a deep feeling of connection to the unseen web of life that links us: to the earth, to the past that shaped us, and to one another.

Dr. Shinichiro Kumagaya offers this insight: "True independence is having many places to depend on." In other words, sustaining multiple sources of connection and diverse networks of support is essential. Those who rely too heavily on one connection can become so dependent that the relationship turns obsessive, often cutting them off from others. This pattern is frequently exploited by cults, which isolate followers from existing ties to create dependency. Conversely, having multiple support systems allows us to have numerous outlets and consider things from different perspectives; it is more balanced and healthy, ensuring that we don't become trapped in a single dependence.

In workplaces, employee engagement scores often measure how well individuals resonate with the company's vision and goals, reflecting workforce motivation and productivity. While high scores in this area may seem positive, they miss the point that work is not our entire life. I encourage people to invest themselves in many areas of living, not just their jobs. Building multiple networks, both professionally and privately, enhances balance and well-being, which I frequently emphasize in career development. For those in leadership, encouraging team members to cultivate diverse forms of support fosters resilience in the workforce.

Recognizing solitude as part of interbeing can provide valuable insights when you are tackling complex issues, particularly if you are in a leadership position. Rather than reinforcing a sense of isolation, solitude becomes a chance to pause, explore different viewpoints, and strengthen genuine connections. By treating solitude as an occasion to deepen mutual relationships, leaders can guide teams through challenges while maintaining a healthy balance of individual reflection and group collaboration.

No matter how alone we might feel at times, the presence of people, plants, animals, and the environment around us sustains and supports us. Life unfolds through our multiple and varied interactions, including those beyond our conscious control, often creating unanticipated connections that can bring about profound joy.

## Does "My Ability" Exist?

In the corporate world, we often think of *ability* as an individual trait—some skill or competence that a person possesses and improves over time. However, if our abilities truly belong to us alone, how do we explain the way an individual's performance can shift so drastically across different environments? This observation suggests that ability is not just a personal attribute, but also depends on the web of relationships and circumstances that we find ourselves in.

From a Buddhist perspective, capability emerges and evolves through our interactions with others and with the wider environment. It's not merely a matter of what we can do by ourselves, but of how our potential unfolds in the presence of people, resources, and opportunities around us, like tree roots spreading into the soil for sustenance.

A diverse project team illustrates this well. Engineers might supply technical know-how, designers contribute creative vision, and marketeers bring strategic insight. No single individual could achieve what they accomplish collectively. The team's success arises from the fusion of their varied strengths, highlighting that genuine growth depends on recognizing "our collective ability," not just "my personal ability."

When we recognize ability as a collective phenomenon, professional development becomes less about each person running their own race and more about sharing a collective path. Leaders can foster an environment where people's strengths thrive through communal experiences and mutual support, reinforcing the truth that we flourish by both giving and receiving from the group's shared pool of talent and knowledge. In this sense, rethinking success as an expression of interdependence prompts growth that benefits not just the individual but also the wider workplace collective.

Buddhist teachings remind us that boundless potential exists within every being. If we want to call that potential *ability*, then perhaps we need to reframe it from "my ability" to "our ability," flowing from the connections among us all.

## The Pitfalls of Incentives and Attachments

In recent years, mindfulness has become increasingly widespread, extending to workplace initiatives that promote well-being. At its core, mindfulness is about moving away from attachment, fostering a state of both presence and detachment.

However, even as mindfulness becomes more popular, modern society remains awash with systems that encourage attachment. Our devices bombard us with notifications that spark new wants, creating a perpetual cycle of consumption. This is no accident; it's a deliberate construct that fuels economic growth by pushing continuous demand.

In corporate settings, incentives are often used to boost employee motivation and performance. Though well intentioned, such strategies can exceed natural curiosity and intrinsic drive, venturing into the realm of attachment. This fosters fixation, where incentives become less about inspiration and more about dependency.

Buddhism teaches that the effect of any practice or tool depends on how it is approached. While mindfulness is inherently a practice that moves us away from attachment, when adopted within competitive, incentive-driven frameworks, it risks reinforcing the very attachments it seeks to dissolve. The concept of attachment in the market economy can often become counterproductive when unchecked, blurring the line between motivation and obsession.

Shifting from short-term incentives to deeper, intrinsic fulfillment is essential for creating work-places grounded in genuine mindfulness. When we stop pursuing a superficial happiness rooted in attachment and instead seek to understand suffering and cultivate nonattachment, true wisdom—and genuine happiness—emerges. This cultivation happens not through grand initiatives but through consistent small practices—starting meetings with a moment of shared silence, expressions of authentic gratitude, or brief pauses to reconnect with one's deeper purpose—that gradually shift our relationship to work itself. This wisdom can then reshape organizational mindsets, paving the way for more enduring well-being among employees and within the broader community.

Mindful practice is not solely about individual effort; it's deeply interconnected with how we view our relationships and sense of purpose. In Buddhism, the community of practitioners, *sangha*, is crucial. This collective approach can prompt businesses to think beyond individual gains and examine whether their company culture aligns with shared values among employees and even beyond.

## From Small Desires to Great Aspirations

Some may wonder whether Buddhism, which teaches the letting go of desire, discourages having dreams or goals. Yet, as long as we are human, it is impossible to erase desire entirely. In this light, I recall a temple priest's teaching on moving from "small desires" to "great aspirations."

Small desires are rooted in personal ego and focus only on one's own satisfaction. Great aspirations, on the other hand, stem from a deeper wish that goes beyond the self, aiming for the well-being of both oneself and others. When we concentrate on small, self-centered goals, our thinking can become narrow. By contrast, great aspirations expand our vision, fueling growth and transformation.

How do we nurture such aspirations? Our goals depend on our capacity, and this capacity isn't fixed. It evolves and grows through experiences, relationships, and challenges. In my own work mentoring people in corporate settings, I've seen how genuine development emerges when individuals confront new perspectives that push them to grow.

For instance, I've watched mentees shift from being driven by personal ambition to a collective outlook, changing their measure of success to how they uplift their teams and communities. This broadening of vision is a cornerstone of true leadership development.

Paul Polman, former CEO of Unilever, offers a real-world example. His emphasis on sustainability and shared prosperity, implementing a Sustainable

Living Plan that focused on the health and well-being of employees, showed how a leader's expanded aspiration can spark systemic change that benefits many.

Sometimes, we set goals simply out of necessity or because of external advice. But when we truly internalize those goals, they can turn into deeply personal missions. Through continual effort and reflection, our initial, smaller desires can evolve into large-scale aspirations, embracing others in the process.

Let us not settle for small desires. Instead, let's cultivate great aspirations that intertwine our own development with the greater good.

## Living between Opposites

Many corporate employees, especially those in middle management, find themselves in a state of tension, caught between directives from above and the real-world challenges voiced by their teams. This balancing act often leads to a sense of frustration, with limited time to process the conflicts in play. Casual conversations or after-work socializing may offer brief respite, but in the end, middle managers must make decisions and deliver results, frequently without feeling fully at ease with their choices.

In today's fast-paced, interconnected world, it's increasingly difficult to operate within a single area of expertise. Middle managers, situated between top leadership and frontline workers, contend with cross-departmental communication, client relations, and ethical or societal expectations extending beyond the company's walls. The wide-ranging influences they juggle—which are often contradictory—are inherently complex and challenging to manage.

Although especially evident in middle management, this tension speaks to a more universal reality: in many organizations, and in wider life beyond the workplace, we are often tasked with achieving continuous outcomes on tight deadlines while navigating conflicting pressures. Buddhism addresses this fundamental struggle, framing it as a key aspect of human experience.

In Buddhist thought, *analytical thinking* and *holistic intuition* are central concepts. While analytical thinking is often revered for its clarity and decisiveness, Buddhism highlights that reality is ultimately indivisible. Genuine wisdom calls us to transcend rigid judgments in favor of a holistic viewpoint that perceives the interconnected whole, free from binary constraints.

Philosopher Christian Madsbjerg, in his book *Look*, underscores the importance of observing without immediately judging. He posits that such a capacity helps leaders grasp the intricate realities of a situation and, therefore, respond effectively, echoing Buddhism's call to move beyond pure analysis and witness the deeper, intertwined nature of problems.

When middle managers or others feel trapped by opposing demands, they can reframe their situation as a form of practice, a chance to engage with the "unresolvable" and seek genuine understanding. In a world where circumstances grow ever more complex, we benefit from learning to occupy this middle ground with openness, evolving beyond routine problem-solving toward a more profound comprehension of reality.

## Embracing the Unknown

In today's rapidly changing business landscape, leaders often encounter situations where clear answers are elusive. Navigating these conditions requires a mindset that aligns with the middle way of Buddhist philosophy—a willingness to live in the space between certainty and uncertainty. In recent years, there has been increasing emphasis on concepts such as *negative capability*, which refers to staying composed amid ambiguity, and *paradoxical leadership*, which centers on managing contradictions. Both reflect the essence of the middle way: rather than choosing definitively between two extremes, one continuously balances multiple perspectives.

A telling example is found in strategic decision-making. Leaders may face market shifts that don't, in fact, call for immediate, definitive solutions. Instead of hastily labeling or resolving these issues, it can be more effective to pause, observe, and allow the team to adapt over time. This "watchful waiting" demands skill in the form of nonjudgmental observation, a vital competence for leaders who aim to respond thoughtfully instead of reacting on impulse.

Humans naturally crave clarity. Our brains are wired to categorize and analyze and, through this process, assign meaning to the world. While this aptitude helps us solve problems and navigate social structures, it can also trap us in habitual patterns. Leaders who ask themselves, "Am I truly perceiving the situation in front of me, or am I filtering it through my past experiences and biases?" invite more open-ended exploration and deeper insight.

Collaboration invariably involves working through conflict and ambiguity, whether that's in boardrooms, classrooms, family interactions, or personal reflections. Recognizing ourselves as interbeing, thriving amid contradictions, embodies the middle way. While navigating paradoxes can be uncomfortable, it also offers the potential for substantial personal and organizational growth. Rather than eliminating contradictions, the path forward is to accept them as integral to the leadership journey.

## The Pitfalls of Altruism

Practicing genuine altruism can be challenging. When we feel a selfless intention—*I'm doing this for them*—we may be disappointed if it's not received in the way we hoped. Suddenly, what felt like the Buddha within us transforms into frustration—*But I did this for you!* We need to pause whenever we notice words like *but* or *yet* creeping into our thoughts or speech.

In truth, our existence depends on interconnected relationships with other people and other living beings. The self cannot be entirely separated from others. Even at this moment, as you read this, the air you breathe becomes part of your body. Life is an infinite, ever-shifting web of relationships, of giving and receiving. The Buddhist teaching of "benefiting self and others harmoniously" is not merely a slogan, but a mirror of the interconnected reality we inhabit.

When we consciously think *I'm being altruistic*, we risk imposing our will on others without meaning to. Sometimes, this comes across as overbearing or even hurtful. The more we emphasize our altruism, the more we might expect gratitude or acknowledgment, unintentionally creating an imbalance, a giver-receiver dynamic that can resemble a power structure.

True altruism flows naturally, forming a reciprocal circle of mutual benefit. If this circle is broken, altruism can become one-sided. Even when work is intrinsically good, authentic altruism operates beyond our immediate awareness. The "altruistic" world we perceive can be narrow in scope.

Consider building a habit of making small actions—an encouraging word to a colleague, for instance—that can nonetheless significantly boost morale or team spirit and which, over time, becomes subconscious. In this way, altruistic acts can extend beyond our conscious intentions.

In my own work, mentoring leaders at various organizations, I've seen how embracing altruism by nurturing others—without expecting immediate returns—reflects the heart of so-called servant leadership. This approach fosters the growth of others, ultimately benefiting the collective and strengthening communal well-being.

It's crucial, though, to remain open, giving others space to accept or reject our efforts as they wish. After all, we can never truly know what someone else wants.

## Happiness for the Whole

"There is no such thing as individual happiness until the entire world is happy."

This profound line comes from the renowned Japanese poet and writer Kenji Miyazawa.

Many people might assume that if all individuals were to achieve happiness, then the world as a whole would naturally follow. This idea echoes modern philosophy rooted in nineteenth-century thinkers like Jeremy Bentham, who championed "the greatest happiness of the greatest number"—a view that treats each person as a single unit that contributes to a collective well-being.

However, Buddhism consistently questions the notion that happiness can be compartmentalized into separate individuals. Texts like the *Heart Sutra* use repeated negations (*no* or *non-*) to emphasize that all existence is fundamentally interwoven. The idea of interdependence, or interbeing, underlines how individuals exist only in relation to others and the world at large. In this view, any attempt to isolate one person's happiness from the broader web of life is merely a convenient illusion.

Miyazawa's deep commitment to the teachings of the *Lotus Sutra* suggests that he viewed personal and global happiness as inseparably linked. Neither can exist without the other. His words challenge us to reconsider what it means to pursue happiness in a universe where nothing, and no one, truly stands alone.

Modern-day examples of this outlook can be found in companies like Patagonia, which famously declared, "The Earth is now our only shareholder," and puts 100 percent of the company's excess profits (profit after reinvestment in the company) into environmental causes, underscoring a purpose beyond simply generating profit. Likewise, benefit corporations (B Corps) measure the company's success according to their positive impact on society and their environment, reflecting a move away from purely individualistic aims and toward collective well-being.

Miyazawa's message endures as a reminder that our individual happiness is tied to the happiness of all. Embracing this interconnected perspective leads us to think not only of our own fulfillment, but of the flourishing of the entire world.

## Impermanence as the Core of Business Evolution

In today's organizations, diversity, equity, and inclusion have become central values, which means that within a single company, people of varying backgrounds, ages, roles, skills, and perspectives coexist. The necessary friction that arises from this intermingling can be seen in longtime employees reminiscing about a past with looser management and less competition, while those who joined from other firms may recall more flexible work cultures and feel restricted in their new roles.

Such comparisons—between past and present, or

among different corporate environments—reveal our innate struggle with change. We want stability but also crave improvement, creating inner conflict. This longing often surfaces as, "It shouldn't be this way," fueling a sense of dissatisfaction.

Yet Buddhism reminds us that everything is in constant flux—a principle known as impermanence. In Japanese culture, *shogyō mujō*—the principle that everything is impermanent—shapes many traditions, such as the annual viewing of the cherry blossoms, a seasonal celebration of life's fleeting beauty. This focus on, and celebration of, the transience of all things urges us to appreciate the present moment. The centering of impermanence in these traditions highlights that transformation is not an external phenomena but an intrinsic part of existence. As Heraclitus famously put it, "Change is the only constant."

Leaders who accept impermanence can more readily adapt new strategies and cultivate resilience in evolving business landscapes. IBM offers one such example: once focused on physical machines, the company has steadily reinvented itself—from hardware to AI—to remain aligned with shifting markets. For a company such as this, adaptation is not optional, but essential for longevity.

Accepting change means not just adjusting external practices, but also recognizing the internal shifts required to stay aligned. It involves listening to our reactions and recalibrating our mindsets and actions in response. True growth does not come from chasing every new trend, but from staying attuned to the subtle, internal cues that mirror the flow of external change.

Both individuals and organizations are subject to impermanence. Attempts to freeze the status quo rarely result in long-term viability. True resilience emerges when we accept change as a vital ally rather than viewing it as an adversary, fostering continuous evolution and renewal.

It may also explain why Japan, which embraces impermanence at its cultural core, has a remarkable concentration of centuries-old companies that continue to thrive as a result of this adaptability and resilience.

### Awakening and *Ikigai*

Some may worry that attaining awakening would erode motivation or diminish the drive to succeed. However, such concerns are unfounded. Awakening does not negate one's sense of *ikigai*, or life purpose.

When Gautama Buddha experienced awakening at age thirty-five, he initially hesitated to share his profound realization. The *dharma* he had discovered was subtle and deep, difficult for others to comprehend. He contemplated whether it might be better to dwell peacefully in his newfound wisdom rather than attempt to teach it to others. But according to tradition, Brahma Sahampati, a deity symbolizing creation and guidance, appeared before Gautama Buddha and implored him to share his insights for the benefit of all beings who were seeking truth.

This was a pivotal moment in Buddhism and has much to teach us about one of the most crucial forms of leadership, where the urge to impart wisdom surpasses personal gain. Gautama Buddha's decision foregrounded the role of those mentors who guide others to move beyond individual fulfillment and toward broader contributions.

Recognizing that awakening did not mean the end of endeavor, Buddha devoted the next forty-five years of his life to alleviating *dukkha* and cultivating joy in others. While *dukkha* is often interpreted as "suffering," it can also describe a friction or misalignment in one's life path. This friction is not necessarily harmful and can stimulate growth and spark transformation.

Far from being a barrier to motivation, awakening allows one to pursue actions free from excessive attachment. With a diminished fear of loss, individuals are able to engage with the present moment genuinely and invest their energies into meaningful endeavors without being swayed by transient noise.

## Chapter 4

# We Become Buddha

## People's Buddhism in Times of Crisis

Three years had passed since I first started visiting the mountain temple. There's a saying: "If you sit on a cold rock for three years, it warms up." In this way, the teachings of the temple seemed to have quietly settled into my life. The work I do in organizational development used to feel uncertain and confusing, but over time, I was learning to let things be. I came to trust that clarity would arrive on its own schedule. In today's terms, maybe I had become a bit better at living with uncertainty and reflecting on my own thoughts.

Then, one day, this calm routine was shattered.

I felt slightly ill and went to the doctor for a quick checkup. It turned into an urgent exam, and before I knew it, I was told I had cancer.

Events like serious illness, accidents, or natural disasters strike suddenly, without warning. In an instant, all the minor "life noise" that had once bothered me vanished. In that strange silence, it felt as though the solid ground beneath my feet had split open, and I was falling into darkness. Questions rushed in: *What about my family? What about my work? What does it mean to live or die? Does my life have any real purpose?*

When the usual noise of daily life fades, we're forced to confront what truly matters.

I once heard a cancer survivor describe the feeling like this:

*Imagine you're on a bus with friends, happily heading toward a shared destination. Suddenly, you alone are told to get off at the next stop. You don't want to leave, but you have no choice. You say goodbye, step off the bus, and watch it drive away, leaving you alone at the bus stop. Can you imagine that feeling?*

In the wake of a life-altering shock such as a cancer diagnosis, the everyday noise—the work stress, the small worries, the busy hum of life—continues to be a part of being alive. But behind that everyday world lies another dimension where all noise disappears. In that silent realm, you face a reality you cannot change. Choices fall away, leaving only the feeling of helplessness as you stand face-to-face with your inner turmoil.

During the years that I had visited the temple, I had learned that mindfulness is found not only in formal meditation, but also in simple daily acts: cleaning, chanting *sutras*, greeting others. These practices, woven into our People's Buddhism, had increasingly helped ground me in the present. I thought I had fully integrated these teachings into my home and work life. But now, facing my cancer diagnosis, I couldn't work or live as before. Even visiting the temple wouldn't be the same. In this crisis, I wondered how Buddhism could guide me.

When I reached out to the temple, the priest kindly offered to spend three days with me, sharing his teachings. With just a week left before I went into the hospital for treatment, I set out once more to the mountain temple, hoping that People's Buddhism could anchor me in this profound moment of uncertainty.

### Helpless

The temple priest greeted me with a gentle "Welcome back." We sat across from each other in the quiet hall. Behind him stood the life-size statue of Amida Buddha. As I settled down, memories of my first visit to this temple came back to me, washing over me like déjà vu.

I thanked the priest for making time to see me and spoke from my heart: "Priest, I'm grateful for the teachings you've shared with me over the years. Your lessons on People's Buddhism helped me handle my busy, often chaotic life at home and at work. I thought I understood your saying that 'the ordinary and the extraordinary sit side by side,' but now that I face an illness that touches the core of life itself, I see that I never truly grasped it. We move through our daily lives surrounded by noise, not realizing that a crisis may lie just beyond it. Only when that everyday noise disappears are we forced to face reality. Could you share the Buddha's teachings with me again? I feel helpless. Until now, I had believed that my career and my life were built upon my own choices—upon my own 'agency.' But in the face of this illness, that very feeling has crumbled away, and the illusion of my control has vanished completely.'"

The priest listened quietly, then spoke in a gentle voice:

> *"Everything that happens in our lives is shaped by karmic conditions, the web of causes and effects that connects us all. Illness, injuries, troubles at work or at home, the loss of loved ones, wars,*

earthquakes, tsunamis, typhoons, wildfires—any of these can arise from the conditions we share.

"When we face a harsh reality we cannot avoid, we can feel overwhelmed and helpless. Yet everyday life is always linked to something beyond the ordinary, beyond the individual self. People's Buddhism, with its focus on being mindful and truly listening, grew from the way we live together, side by side with those who came before us.

"Whether you feel joy or sorrow, these emotions arise from your experience in the moment folded between the past and the present. Still, here we are, alive at this very moment. This is why it's so important to treasure each day. Even when life feels unbearable, even when countries fall into chaos, the sun rises again. Beginning the day with simple, steady routines can renew our spirit and give us the strength we need. Any day can become a good day, depending on how we face it.

"When we confront what seems impossible to solve, mindful listening becomes especially important. Among our senses, hearing often lasts the longest, even when other abilities fail. Even if we can't walk, sit up, speak, read, or see, we may still be able to listen. In those moments of deepest helplessness, that is when the Buddha's voice finally can be heard."

## Leaving the Noisy World, Longing for a Serene, Pure Land

What does *becoming Buddha* mean?

*"Becoming Buddha means having a mind that stays calm and steady, no matter what happens around you. We only experience something as noise when we label it that way. The Buddha represents a state free from all noise, a true stillness of the heart. Though this might sound lofty, it is not something distant and unreachable. It exists right here, right now—so close that we often need to take an unexpected route to notice it.*

*"In Buddhism, the wish to become a Buddha is called the 'intention to awaken.' It marks the beginning of our path toward wisdom.*

*"Even people who meditate every day may never say to themselves 'I want to become a Buddha.' Yet almost everyone has felt the urge to escape the endless distractions and find a place of peace.*

*"This feeling is expressed by the phrase 'Leaving the noisy world, longing for a serene, pure land.'*

*"This phrase means wishing to leave behind our noise-filled world and be 'reborn' into a peaceful, pure realm where it's easy to become Buddha.*

*The idea guided figures like Tokugawa Ieyasu, the seventeenth-century shōgun who helped bring about a long era of peace in Japan after years of conflict.*

*"In today's world, with so many distractions overwhelming our senses, the desire to step away from chaos and discover serenity is something most of us will understand.*

*"We may have articulated the thought, 'I want to become Buddha,' but when we long to leave noise behind and find quiet, we're already starting on the path of Nen Buddhism, taking the first steps toward a practice focused on mindful listening and thoughtful reflection.*

*"When Gautama Siddhartha faced life's unavoidable truths—birth, aging, sickness, and death—he set off on his own journey, driven by the same desire: to step away from the noisy world and seek a calm, peaceful existence."*

## Gautama Siddhartha and Gautama Buddha

*"Gautama Buddha's life takes us back about twenty five hundred years, to ancient India, where Buddhism began.*

*"Gautama Siddhartha was born a prince. Al-*

though he enjoyed a privileged life, he could not ignore the basic hardships all humans face: birth, aging, sickness, and death. At twenty-nine, he left his family and social position behind, choosing a life of strict practice to seek answers to these problems.

"He carried a sincere wish—'I want to become Buddha'—and worked very hard at his practice.

"At the time when Siddhartha set out on his path, 'becoming Buddha' was not yet an established or widely recognized goal—he was the first to define and personify that very aspiration.

"After six years, at the age of thirty-five, he reached a state of ultimate awakening and became Buddha, the 'Awakened One.' From then on, until he passed away at eighty, he spent the remaining years of his life helping many others find their own path to awakening.

"When Gautama Siddhartha became Gautama Buddha, he experienced a significant change. After achieving his long-held goal—'I want to become Buddha'—he asked himself, 'Now that I've done this, what should I do next?' Some stories say he felt an inner doubt or voice suggesting things like 'You've reached the highest point; maybe no one else will understand,' or 'Since you've already succeeded, why continue?' But instead of stopping, he made a new promise: 'I will help others reach this calm and pure state, too.' This marked his new vow: 'We become Buddha.'

"Over his lifetime, Gautama moved from a personal aim—'I want to become Buddha'—to a shared vow—'We become Buddha.' Early on, he relied on his own effort, but later he focused on guiding everyone toward awakening. Compassion was at the center of this work.

"Buddha's approach to helping others always began with listening. Then he would adjust his teachings to suit each person's needs. It was akin to how a doctor listens to a patient before giving advice. In this way, Buddha shows us the importance of truly hearing others."

## Gautama or Buddha

"Buddhism is the path through which I become Buddha.

"You may wonder if there is only one path, or if there are many. Around the world, Buddhism naturally divided into two main streams: Theravada and Mahayana. Theravada Buddhism spread across parts of Southeast Asia, such as Thailand and Sri Lanka, while Mahayana Buddhism took root in East Asia, including Japan.

*"The key difference between them lies in which aspect of Gautama Buddha's story they emphasize. Theravada focuses on Gautama Siddhartha, the historical individual who achieved awakening. Mahayana focuses on Buddha, the potential for enlightenment that all beings share.*

*"In Theravada Buddhism, the spotlight is on Gautama's personal journey. When Siddhartha began his quest, 'Buddhism' as a system did not yet exist. He walked the path alone, relying on his own strength. At the age of thirty-five, he attained awakening and became the very first Buddha in history. Theravada Buddhists hold this event in high regard and adopt the vow 'I want to become Buddha, too,' aiming to follow Gautama's example. Those who have attained enlightenment after hearing Gautama's teachings are called 'voice hearers,' since they reached understanding by listening directly to him.*

*"Mahayana Buddhism, on the other hand, sees 'Buddha' not just as one historical figure, but as a universal potential that anyone can realize. Gautama himself hinted at this when he said, 'Abandon the raft once you have crossed the river,' urging people not to cling to the form of his teachings. In Mahayana, the focus shifts from 'I want to become Buddha' to 'We become Buddha,' reminding us that everyone can share in this potential.*

*"Both traditions converge on the same core: awakening as an inherent capacity in all beings— the path of actually becoming Buddha, which is the essence of Buddhism."*

## Who Can Become Buddha?

Is it only human beings who can become Buddha?

*"Within Buddhism there is the concept of 'sentient beings,' which refers to any living creature that can feel pain and suffering. Some Buddhist traditions in Japan say that if a being can experience suffering, it can also become a Buddha. This means not only humans but also animals like dogs or cats hold the potential for enlightenment.*

*"In the People's Buddhism that developed in Japan, we took this view even further. We came to believe that not only living creatures but also things we usually consider nonliving carry the possibility of becoming Buddha. We say that 'mountains, rivers, and all things can attain Buddhahood.' This reminds us to listen mindfully to all existence, not just what we perceive as alive. This outlook expands the range of what we recognize as capable of awakening.*

*"People often ask, 'Do I have to become a monk to attain Buddhahood?' The answer is no.*

*Becoming a monk is a human-made rule. Since even nonhuman beings can become Buddha, becoming a monk is not a requirement.*

*"Our People's Buddhism focuses on the 'person,' the source of a voice. Humans, animals, and all things have their own ways of expressing themselves. If ordaining as a monk helps you find your true voice, that's fine. If not, you can stay as you are. Either way, you are free to walk the path.*

*"You may be familiar with Zen Buddhism from Japan. Long ago, a master named Dōgen chose a quiet mountain area to build Eiheiji Temple, so monks could focus on meditation without distractions. Some Zen temples in busy towns also try to reduce external noise, and some do not allow visitors for this reason. Traditional Zen training often suited those who could devote their entire day to practice in a peaceful place.*

*"But not everyone can live like that. Most ordinary people, like you and me, are busy with daily responsibilities. We may never have the time or chance to enter a special training hall. Or we may have tried, struggled, and given up.*

*"So, is there a path for ordinary people, surrounded by daily noise, within which they can find calm and become Buddha? This question led to the development of various new Buddhist paths, including Nen Buddhism.*

*"Tomorrow, I will tell you more about Nen Buddhism."*

I thought about what it meant for someone like me, currently feeling so helpless, to walk the path to becoming Buddha. I wanted to follow the example of Gautama Buddha, but the path he walked seemed so far away, especially as I felt my time and energy running low. Knowing there was a way for ordinary people like me to move toward becoming Buddha made me feel both anxious and hopeful.

Carrying these mixed feelings, I left the temple after the first day of the priest's teachings.

## Nen Buddhism

The following day, I returned to the temple hall. Once again, it was just the temple priest and me. I settled in, hoping to feel closer to Buddha.

The priest began to speak:

*"At the root of our People's Buddhism are two important figures: Hōnen and Shinran. About eight hundred fifty years ago, at a time when many believed Buddhism belonged only to monks, Hōnen rediscovered and revitalized an ancient tradition of practice that was open to all, no matter if you were monastic or lay, male or*

*female, rich or poor. This path, known as Nen Buddhism, had existed long before, but it was Hōnen who made it accessible to ordinary Japanese people as a practice that could be lived out in everyday life.*

*"Shinran, who followed Hōnen, described himself as 'neither monastic nor secular' and moved away from traditional monastic roles. He lived as a layperson, raising a family and practicing Nen Buddhism in ordinary life.*

*"From this tradition came many remarkable lay followers called* myōkōnin, *people who practice Buddhism while living and working like everyone else. They are 'awakened laypersons' who show that genuine spiritual growth can occur in daily life, not only in temples or through formal practices.*

*"D. T. Suzuki, who introduced Zen Buddhism to the wider world, was also a devoted follower of Nen Buddhism and deeply respected the lives of the* myōkōnin. *Although it may be less well known globally, Nen Buddhism actually has more followers in Japan than Zen Buddhism does."*

Zen (禅) and Nen (念)—even the sounds seem similar. So how is Nen Buddhism different from Zen Buddhism?

*"Zen Buddhism focuses on* shikantaza, *which means "just sitting" with complete concentration. The idea is to become one with the act of sitting, straightening your back, and clearing your mind, like an empty vessel through which everything can flow freely.*

*"In contrast, Nen Buddhism could be described as 'just listening.' In Nen Buddhism, we value listening wholeheartedly. Not only with our ears, but by emptying our hearts, becoming like an open vessel that accepts sound fully. This is what it means to truly embody listening."*

### "Naam Aami Daab"

*"To engage in Nen Buddhism practice, we often chant a sound known as 'Naam Aami Daab.'*

*"These words come from six Kanji characters, '南無阿弥陀佛,' but we usually break them into three syllables: 'Naam,' 'Aami,' and 'Daab.' Together, these three sounds form a rhythm. They include the 'aum' sound, starting with 'a' and ending with 'um,' repeated in a gentle three-beat cycle.*

*"In Nen Buddhism, we repeat this phrase as a central practice. Many people in East Asia will have heard 'Naam Aami Daab,' but not everyone knows what it signifies.*

*"Does 'Naam Aami Daab' have a meaning? In one sense, yes. The 'Nam,' similar to 'namaste,' shows reverence and an openness of the heart toward the Buddha. 'Aami Daab' is linked to a Buddha named Amida, whose name comes from a word meaning 'immeasurable.' This suggests a Buddha with unmeasurable light and life—what we might call 'Unmeasurable Buddha.' It represents a space and time that leave no one behind.*

*"On the other hand, if we think about it differently, 'Naam Aami Daab' can simply be seen as sound. The characters mostly serve as a way to represent the voice. When we chant 'Naam Aami Daab,' we do not need to focus on the meaning; we can just listen to the sound. This allows us to let go of the constant search for understanding, much like sitting in silent meditation without chasing after our thoughts.*

*"Even though we cannot see it, the vow 'We become Buddha' quietly echoes throughout the universe. These six characters remind us that we are all on a path to becoming Buddha. Taken simply, it means 'We become Buddha.' If we look deeper, we find a rich story around Amida Buddha and the promise of awakening.*

*"In this way, 'Naam Aami Daab' is both sim-*

*ple and profound. By trusting in these sounds and letting them fill our hearts, we connect directly with the Buddha's voice, free from the weight of complicated thoughts."*

## The Middle Voice

*"If mindful listening is at the heart of Nen Buddhism, you might wonder why we focus on chanting the name of Amida Buddha.*

*"The essence of Nen Buddhism can be summed up as: 'Listen mindfully, then the voice will be heard.' But this raises a question: How are 'listening' and 'hearing' related?*

*"Earlier, I said that the Buddha's vow shifted from 'I want to become Buddha' to 'We become Buddha.' This change reflects moving away from a small, self-focused viewpoint toward an open awareness of our shared existence. It is a shift from 'I listen' to 'The voice is heard.'*

*"In Buddhism, we often talk about moving from seeing things as separate and divided to experiencing them as connected and whole. Nen Buddhism uses the element of voice to guide us through this change, helping us move from a mindset of 'me' and 'you' to one where all beings are linked together.*

*"If you have ever studied ancient languages, you may have heard of the 'middle voice.' Some old languages had forms of verbs that were not active (like 'I love') or passive (like 'I am loved'), but somewhere in between. In this middle voice, the subject becomes a space where the action happens, without force or control. For example, if we think about 'love,' in English we say 'I love you,' suggesting active effort on the part of the first person. But love often arises on its own; it simply appears, without conscious decision. Some languages once had a way of linguistically expressing this natural, effortless state of love.*

*"Nen Buddhism uses chanting to bring us into this state, where active and passive blend into one. By chanting, we start to drop the habits of language that divide us into 'doer' and 'done-to.' As we continue, we move from seeing the world as separate parts to feeling it as a whole. In other traditions like Zen, people use kōans, riddles that cannot be solved by logic, to break free from the structures of everyday thinking. In Nen Buddhism, chanting 'Naam Aami Daab' serves a similar purpose: it carries us beyond words, even though we are using words."*

What actually changes when we chant?

*"At first, maybe nothing seems different. Chanting does not magically make the world clearer or our hearts pure overnight. But in Nen Buddhism, we learn that waiting is important. We do not force ourselves to hear the voice; instead, we trust that if we keep listening and chanting, the voice will come to us in its own time. I have noticed that through chanting, my ability to accept whatever comes grows deeper.*

*"You could say: 'If we chase the path, it runs away, but if we wait with trust, it draws near.'*

*"Let's end our talk here for today."*

After saying this, the temple priest turned toward the Amida Buddha statue.

*"Naam Aami Daab, Naam Aami Daab . . ."*

His calm voice filled the hall.

On my way home, I tried quietly chanting to myself: *"Naam Aami Daab, Naam Aami Daab . . ."*

Nothing dramatic happened. I felt no sudden insight or sensation.

*"Listen mindfully, then the voice will be heard."*

That's what the priest said.

## The Story of Amida Buddha

It was the final day of my talk with the priest before I was admitted to the hospital. The priest entered the temple hall, faced the statue of Buddha, and gently pressed his palms together. The golden figure that had witnessed all of our conversations was not Gautama Buddha, the historical founder of Buddhism, but Amida Buddha, the central figure of devotion in Nen Buddhism and the focus of the chanting practice we had discussed. In a calm voice, the temple priest chanted:

*"Naam Aami Daab, Naam Aami Daab . . ."*

He repeated this chant ten times.

I had been told to listen for the Buddha's voice, but I still couldn't sense it. Could the priest actually hear it? Unsure of what I was missing, I folded my arms and focused on what he would say next.

He gestured at the Buddha statue that had been present for so many of our conversations and began.

*"This is Amida Buddha.*

*"Chanting the name of Amida Buddha unfolds a vast story. Let me share with you the tale as described in the* sutras. *Long ago, there was a* bodhisattva—*a person devoted to the path of be-*

coming Buddha—highly respected in Mahayana Buddhism for caring about the well-being of all living things.

"This bodhisattva once encountered a Buddha and felt so inspired that he vowed, 'I want to become Buddha.' But his goal went beyond his own awakening. He promised, 'I will never become Buddha unless I can help every being, every creature that lives and breathes, reach Buddhahood as well.' In other words, he made a vow of 'We become Buddha.'

"This is not the same vow that Gautama Buddha made earlier in the history of Buddhism; rather, it is the 'original vow' of the bodhisattva who would later become Amida Buddha, a vow formulated and recorded in Mahayana sutras centuries after Gautama's enlightenment.

"Over an immeasurably long time, this bodhisattva completed his practice and achieved awakening, thus becoming Buddha himself. He took the name Amida Buddha, embodying the vow to guide all beings to awakening. The name Amida Buddha comes from amitabha (boundless light) and amitayus (boundless life), suggesting an endless reach across space and time, making sure no one is left behind.

"By hearing Amida Buddha's story and continuing the practice of calling, we gradually see *more clearly that 'We become Buddha.' The name Amida Buddha symbolizes the completion of this collective vow.*

*"This vow, often called the 'original vow,' represents a deep connection passed down through countless generations—from those who came before us to those not yet born. The word 'original' comes from the Latin* origo, *meaning 'beginning' but also 'source,' which suggests not just a starting point, but a continuous lineage, an ongoing call shared by past, present, and future to awaken together.*

*"In these teachings, Amida Buddha's realm is known as the 'Pure Land,' a place where anyone who seeks it can become Buddha without any barriers.*

*"That, in essence, is the story."*

## How Can We Meet an Unseen Buddha?

Looking at the statue of Amida Buddha behind the priest, I wondered if he was a historical figure.

*"No. While Gautama Buddha, who was originally born Siddhartha Gautama, is known to be a historical figure who lived and attained Buddhahood, Amida Buddha appears only in stories found in the* sutras.*"*

I asked if that meant Amida Buddha was just imaginary.

*"In one sense, yes.*

*"But consider this: even though Gautama Buddha was once alive, he passed away about twenty-five hundred years ago. If we define 'existing' as something or someone we can touch or see right now, then Gautama Buddha no longer 'exists' in that way. We cannot meet him directly or ask him questions face-to-face.*

*"Yet his teachings have reached us in many forms, and through them, our lives continue to be shaped. By calling his name and carrying on his teachings, we allow Gautama Buddha's voice to resonate in the present moment, influencing how we live right now.*

*"After Gautama Buddha's passing, Mahayana Buddhism arose from a deep desire to understand how we might still encounter a Buddha we cannot see. This longing encouraged followers to think more broadly about how Buddhas might appear, not only in the past but also far into the future. They wondered if many Buddhas came before Gautama Buddha and if many more would emerge long after. Each Buddha, though equally enlightened, might have unique qualities shaped by their different backgrounds. Within these*

*limitless possibilities, Amida Buddha's story stands out as a Buddha whose very purpose is to guide all beings toward awakening.*

*"A story in a book is not truly 'alive' just by existing as text on a page. It gains meaning and power when it inspires people, changes how they see the world, and leads them to act. That's where its real worth lies. Mahayana Buddhism evolved as a living movement, where we bring words to life by practicing them, where we let words nourish us, and where we eventually learn to go beyond the words themselves. As we pursue this ongoing, active engagement, the deeper meanings of the teachings and their influence on our lives come into view."*

## Polyphony of Interbeing

*"In Theravada Buddhism, I mentioned that disciples who attained enlightenment by hearing Gautama Buddha's teachings were called voice hearers. Similarly, Mahayana Buddhism explored a new direction: How can we hear the Buddha's voice after he is no longer physically here? How can everyone become a voice hearer? Instead of focusing only on the single voice of Gautama Buddha, Mahayana encourages us to listen for the po-*

*tential of Buddhahood in all beings—including you and me."*

So, how do we engage in this listening?

*"Especially in the past, before the era of voice recorders, microphones, or speakers, 'meeting' someone was essentially the same as 'exchanging voices.'*

*"It's a process of call-and-response. Just as pouring a little water into a pump draws out the clear spring water below, we first send out our words into the world, before receiving any in return. In Nen Buddhism, the sound 'Naam Aami Daab, Naam Aami Daab,' inspired by the name of Amida Buddha, has been passed down as this initial call. Over countless generations, people have chanted these words, expressing the wish to leave the noisy world behind and seek a serene, pure land.*

*"This longing for a pure realm doesn't mean rejecting the present world entirely, but rather finding a way to experience serenity even amid daily noise—a paradox at the heart of People's Buddhism that embraces both transcendence and engagement with the world as it is.*

*"Once spoken, sound waves travel through the*

*air, causing subtle vibrations. Over time, these waves fade beyond what our ears can detect, but that doesn't mean they vanish completely. If we think about it, every voice ever spoken may still linger in the universe, resonating together to form a deep, continuous note, a polyphony created by all who came before us.*

*"Once we have truly heard this, we cannot forget it. Shinran said that Amida Buddha's work 'even chases after those who try to run away.' This means that no matter who we are or how our world changes, there remains a final path to becoming Buddha."*

## Wholehearted Acceptance

How can Nen Buddhism give us peace of mind during a life crisis? How does it address the deep suffering that comes from birth, aging, illness, and death? Even if we chant "We become Buddha," we may not feel any closer to becoming a Buddha ourselves. Will the day ever come when our suffering ends?

*"Nen Buddhism teaches that while 'We become Buddha' is a promise, it never says exactly when this will happen. It also doesn't limit this process to our present lifetime. In fact, it suggests that our*

*rebirth into the Pure Land of Amida Buddha,
where we will surely become Buddhas, takes
place after this life is over."*

I wondered, if we attain this state only after
death, then what's the point in practicing Buddhism
in the here and now? Is "We become Buddha" just a
comforting phrase? For those of us who struggle
with waiting, these are natural doubts.

*"What Nen Buddhism values most is that the
call of 'We become Buddha' is truly heard and
received clearly and fully in our hearts. This experience is a kind of wholehearted acceptance,
surrendering ourselves to something beyond our
own efforts, finding calm without doubt. This isn't
a passive belief in something distant, but an active trust in the very flow of life that carries us,
even when we feel most helpless.*

*"Nen Buddhism does not grow from the mind-
set of 'I want to become Buddha.' Instead, as we
listen to the call of 'We become Buddha,' this
wholehearted acceptance takes root naturally.
This process is beyond our personal control, and
even if our aspiration to become Buddha is not
met in this lifetime, we can still view all events as
part of the Buddha's working.*

*"When we listen deeply to the Buddha's voice, what comes to us is this wholehearted acceptance. To receive it, we have no choice but to wait. And if we must wait, why not wait with joyful antici-pation? With this approach, let's continue our mindful listening.*

*"The Buddhist path has no end, much like cleaning, which is never truly finished. That means it's never too early or too late to begin walking this path."*

## The Reflection

The temple priest paused, looked directly at me, brought his palms together, and quoted a well-known teaching by Hōnen, the master of Nen Buddhism, in a clear, steady voice:

*"Without trying to appear wise, simply devote yourself to Nen."*

He then turned toward the statue of Amida Buddha and began to chant:

*"Naam Aami Daab, Naam Aami Daab . . ."*

I joined in, and our voices overlapped, echoing softly through the mountain temple.

Nothing dramatic happened. I didn't feel anything particularly striking. Yet, somehow, I felt less anxious, and my heart was calmer than it had been the day before. I still didn't fully understand the Buddha or this path, but at that moment, I realized that it was fine not to have all the answers.

As I walked away from the temple, I reflected on this sense of wholehearted acceptance. Maybe it's similar to what we call awe.

The researcher Dacher Keltner, who studies awe, says this feeling arises when we encounter something so vast or profound that it surpasses our usual understanding. It might be the overwhelming beauty of a wide-open sky or a small, everyday moment that quietly touches your heart. Awe arises when we stop judging or comparing and simply let ourselves be present.

My heart holds awe like soil holds seeds. Sometimes it may feel dry or depleted, but as long as I live, it can still nurture growth. Whether it's a field of sunflowers in rich soil or a single dandelion bravely blooming in the cracked earth, awe does not depend on greatness or perfection. It comes from simply experiencing things as they are.

After learning I was ill, I lost my balance and stopped noticing those small moments of awe in daily life. I had to bring myself back, re-attuning my mind to pick up on them once again. It's like when you stop eating overly spicy food and suddenly rediscover subtle flavors. Calming my mind and tuning in to the gentle scent of trees and the soft breeze, I began to sense the quiet changes in each season once again.

Everything is always changing. Nothing stays the same. And today, right here, I am alive.

## Chapter 5

# The Voice Heard

### Helpless Fool

Many things have happened since that time.

It has been three years since the priest at the mountain temple fell ill and suddenly passed away. Knowing that my memory can fail me, I want to write down the priest's words now, before they fade away.

During the period when I was struggling with my own illness and turning to the temple for comfort, it was the priest who quietly carried my worries. He listened closely to my voice and, in doing so, gave me a part of himself.

In the beginning, I worried not only about my health but also about how my illness would affect my career and finances. Yet, as I grew more familiar with Buddhist teachings, I started to see this unexpected break in my life not as a threat, but as a meaningful gift.

Instead of rejecting or fighting my illness, I began to accept it as something important for my path. This shift reduced much of my stress and may have even helped my recovery.

My cancer is now in remission, and I am in good health.

After the priest passed away, I stopped visiting the temple so often and returned to my job. But sometimes, when I found myself giving advice to people facing career or personal challenges, what I learned from People's Buddhism would come alive again, echoing in the priest's voice, which I can still hear within me.

The priest once told me that in his younger years he lived and trained under strict conditions in a remote monastic environment deep in the mountains. He studied Buddhist teachings and practiced forms of meditation like Zazen, in which you try to clear your mind completely, as the Buddha achieved. He worked very hard, yet no matter how hard he tried, he could not fulfill his vow of "I want to become Buddha." He could not go beyond his human attachments or clear his mind of its troubles. He could not awaken. Feeling a deep sense of failure and helplessness, he left the monastic setting and eventually discovered Nen Buddhism.

Nen Buddhism crosses all boundaries, monastic or not, regardless of social rank, wealth, age, or gender. It invites anyone who wishes to become Buddha to walk that path. The priest often called himself a "fool," probably because he realized during his training that he would never be able to become Buddha through his own efforts. Yet he spoke of this not with bitterness, but with a kind of lightness, saying, "Nen Buddhism is the path that allows helpless fools like me to become Buddha."

Buddhism is not only the teaching of Buddha; it is also the path by which I become Buddha myself. A Buddha is someone who awakens, and this path is my journey toward awakening. But just as we cannot know we are dreaming until we wake up, it is hard to recognize our own confusion while in the midst of living our daily lives.

The Dutch historian Rutger Bregman, in his book *Humankind: A Hopeful History*, questions the often-quoted idea that humans are somehow inherently bad. After carefully reviewing many studies, he concludes that humans are basically "nice fools"—we tend to care about others and show kindness. However, this kindness also makes us easily influenced by outside "noise," and in tough situations, we may lose our sense of humanity.

This resonates with Buddhism, which teaches that humans are inherently fallible and full of contradictions. We are beings with humanness—possessing both kindness and foolishness, compassion and self-centeredness. This beautiful yet complex humanness includes the instinct to protect our own "tribe," which can sometimes make us wary of outsiders.And it is precisely because of this nature that we are included in the path to awakening.

The priest's acceptance of being a "fool" was not negative. He embraced this basic human nature. To be a helpless fool is to be human. To be human is to find joy in stories, art, and the simple beauty of life—things that might no longer touch our hearts if we had already become Buddhas.

Realizing our helplessness is neither about denigrating nor about praising ourselves. It is about seeing human nature for what it is, without labeling it "good" or "bad." Once we see ourselves clearly, we notice our humanness. If we ever lost this imperfection entirely, perhaps we would no longer be human, but already Buddhas.

Nietzsche pointed out our inescapably human limitations in his book *Human, All Too Human*, arguing that wisdom lies in recognizing and embracing our fallibility rather than seeking to transcend it.

It is because we are all too human that we can become Buddha. This is what the temple priest's life always pointed toward.

## A Fool Such as I

The temple priest faced his own helplessness with complete honesty. He often called himself a "fool," not to compare himself with anyone else, but to express a personal truth about his own nature. He never used this term to describe other people, only himself, saying, "A fool such as I."

One day, he said something that made me think deeply:

> *"Even those who rely on self-help can be born into the Pure Land. And, naturally, this also applies to fallible beings who have no self-help at all."*

At first glance, we might think, *If someone without self-help can reach the Pure Land, then surely those who work hard through self-help should find it even easier.* But the priest hinted at a different meaning:

> *"Self-help is closely tied to doubt. It reflects a subtle denial of who we are right now, driven by the wish to become someone else. A fallible being who does not rely on self-help has no doubt. This absence of self-help allows wholehearted acceptance to arise, connecting directly to the Pure Land."*

Perhaps the priest's own past—years of intense training driven by self-help, followed by the painful realization of his unfixable flaws—led him to see things this way. He often spoke of his "stained heart," sometimes telling himself, "Be ashamed, be pitiful for myself." Yet he kept listening: listening to the Buddha's voice, to his own inner voice, and to the voices of others. Following Nen Buddhism, the path of mindful listening, he learned to accept his all-too-human nature.

This path goes beyond labels of "good" or "bad." Consider compassion. It's a beautiful human quality, but the more earnestly we try to be compassionate, the more we notice that our efforts remain limited and self-centered.

Essentially, what the temple priest was pointing out is that I should be more conscious of my habit of unconsciously projecting my own perspective onto others. Here, *others* could mean close family members, a company or society I belong to, animals and plants, or even mountains and rivers.

Granted, the idea of attributing personhood to animals or mountains may stem from good intentions, but it still reflects our "humanness"—an all-too-human way of thinking. Because we humans possess language, we can infinitely expand our circle of imagined "companions" in theory. Yet for each such circle we create, we tend to assume—without even realizing it—that everything within it must share our perspective.

The temple priest's use of "self-centered" did not refer to whether someone is more self-centered than other people; rather, it underscored a universal, all-too-human issue: we simply cannot free ourselves from projecting our own perspective onto others.

In cognitive psychology, this tendency is referred to as *anthropocentric thinking*, meaning the inclination to understand unknown species or processes by drawing analogies with humans. It encompasses a psychological propensity to attribute human characteristics to animals, natural phenomena, and even abstract concepts. People often compare themselves with others, feeling either superior or envious. Yet, the very assumption that one can measure oneself against someone else at all is itself a reflection of our inherently anthropomorphic nature.

As the temple priest noted, it is crucial to be aware of how we unconsciously project our own perspective onto others. Recognizing this habit is the first step toward nurturing a deeper understanding and empathy not only for other people, but also for animals, plants, and the broader natural environment.

Recalling the priest's voice, I remember a gentle sorrow—not despair, but deep empathy and boundless compassion for what it means to be human.

## Medicine and Poison

The temple priest often warned against taking a careless attitude toward being a fool.

> *"While it's true that the Buddha's primal vow includes everyone, this doesn't mean we can behave as we like or become arrogant. Thinking that we can do anything simply because we trust that we will eventually become Buddha is a misunderstanding. This view ignores the fact that every action, good or bad, has consequences that emerge from the web of connections across the Long Now. Even giving up and thinking 'it doesn't matter' contains traces of doubt. Just as having medicine on hand doesn't mean it's okay to drink poison on purpose, we must remain mindful of our actions."*

In Buddhism, the law of *karma* teaches that our actions shape the results we face. This influence extends beyond a single lifetime, reaching across the Long Now of past, present, and future. As humans, we're carried along by forces we never fully understand. Sometimes we harm others without intending to; at other times, we discover ourselves acting kindly in ways that surprise us. Because we are all too human, we often repeat the cycle of "knowing better but doing it again anyway." Yet, within this endless loop lies a chance to grow. Our People's Buddhism does not demand perfection. Instead, it invites *continuous improvement*. It's not about reaching a flawless state, but about seeing our faults and learning from them. Through this ongoing process, we move forward.

## An Entrant of the Irreversible Stream

Nen Buddhism often appeals to people because it shines a light on the difficult parts of human nature. It offers a path not only for those who seem perfect, but for anyone who carries inner struggles. It acknowledges the darkness we hold inside.

There is a saying: "The bigger the 'ice' of our inner impurities, the more 'water' of joy we gain when it melts."

Nen Buddhism shows that suffering can transform into joy, much like a lotus blooming from mud. Yet, even though I practiced mindful listening and chanting, I still had trouble feeling that promised joy. I once confessed these doubts to the temple priest. He replied:

*"I feel the same way.*

*"Sometimes we know we should be joyful, but we can't feel it. This inability to rejoice comes*

*from the tangle of desires and confusion within us—and that's simply part of being human. Yet it is precisely for people like us, who feel helpless, that the immeasurable light of awakening exists. When you think about it this way, doesn't the certainty that we will eventually become Buddha feel even stronger?"*

Nen Buddhism isn't just about trying to become a Buddha right now. It's about realizing that we're already on a sure path toward becoming Buddha. Instead of focusing on "I will become Buddha," we realize, "I am already on an irreversible path toward awakening." For the priest, "We become Buddha" was not a distant goal but something already taking shape within the vast workings of reality. This sense of trust, this wholehearted acceptance, brings calm and peacefulness. It is not forced by our own efforts alone but supported by something larger than ourselves.

Even so, I don't find myself longing to reach the Pure Land immediately. I remain an ordinary person, not yet fully awakened, still human in every way. Yet, by accepting that I'm not there yet, I can see how this greater force gently carries even the helpless toward awakening. It is not about reaching; it is about knowing that I am already carried by an irreversible stream.

## Be Open to the Unknown

Early in my visits to the mountain temple, when I was still looking to Buddhism for a model of living and relying heavily on the priest's guidance, we had this exchange:

*"Do you trust what I say?"*

"Yes, of course," I replied.

*"Then, first, kill a thousand people. If you do that, you can become Buddha."*

Startled, I answered, "I could never do that. I can't even bring myself to kill a mosquito."

*"Exactly. Your ability to act does not rest entirely in your own hands. What you can or cannot do depends on the conditions around you. It's not simply because your heart is good that you do not kill. Under different conditions, people may end up causing the loss of many lives, even without meaning to."*

By using such an extreme example, the temple priest was illustrating that even a good heart alone does not guarantee the right action. External conditions and circumstances can drive people to cause harm, regardless of their intentions. We do not fully understand what is "good" or "evil." The priest always received this truth with a deep sense of sorrow, tempered by acceptance. He was not talking about some future potential for wrongdoing in me or in anyone, but about the harm already caused in ways we do not notice.

> "I know nothing of true good or evil. If I understood goodness as deeply as the Buddha, then I could say I know it. If I understood evil that completely, then I could claim the same. But I do not. I am a helpless fool. This world changes as quickly as a house on fire. Everything I see is fleeting and illusive. Nothing is a permanent truth. I cannot depend on myself or on others. My only refuge is the path of Nen."

We often assume we know right from wrong and believe those who fail to see it are not fit for society. This leads to a culture of blame, where we judge others and often judge ourselves even more harshly. At work and elsewhere, this can create an atmosphere of fear and avoidance of responsibility.

Yet one of the Buddha's simple teachings, called the "Seven Buddhas' Universal Precept Verse," offers a timeless reminder. When the Chinese poet

Bai Juyi asked the Zen master Dao Lin for the essence of the Buddha's teachings, Dao Lin said: "Do no harm, do good, and purify your mind—this is what all Buddhas teach." Bai Juyi dismissed this as something even a three-year-old could understand. Dao Lin replied, "Yes, even a child can understand it, but even an eighty-year-old finds it hard to practice."

Our path is not about reaching perfection. It is about recognizing that we are not there yet. This sense of "not being there yet" is not a weakness. It is an openness that allows us to learn and grow. Like a sculptor seeing possibilities in a rough block of stone, acknowledging our incompleteness lets us shape and reshape ourselves and, in doing so, continue to help those around us.

## One Call or Many?

The temple priest often uttered the words "Naam Aami Daab." Over a lifetime, how many times did this sound emerge from his lips? At the heart of Nen Buddhism lies mindful listening, and at the heart of that listening lies this sound.

"Should I, too, recite it countless times?" I asked the priest on one occasion.

*"People often ask whether calling out to Amida Buddha should be done just once or many times.*

*But it's not about one approach being better than the other, nor is it a question of having to choose between them."*

At first, this sounded like a riddle, but it pointed to something deeper. My life is not limited to the time from birth to death; it is linked to those who came before me and those who will follow, reaching into the Long Now. At the same time, my life appears here and now as something unique and irreplaceable. Each moment is brief and singular, but is also tied to an endless stream of moments that continue to flow.

We can utter only one voice at a time, and each calling is a once-and-only occurrence. Seen from this perspective, every act of calling is singular—a onetime event. But if we focus on the fact that we keep calling with the same voice, it becomes a sequence—a continuous stream of calls. Whether it's just one call or many depends on how we look at it.

If we force ourselves into a simple one-or-many choice, we risk imagining that there is a fixed, unchanging "I" that exists right now and never shifts. This goes against the Buddhist understanding that all things are constantly changing, interconnected, and without any permanent self.

## No Disciple

The temple priest often said he had no disciples. Hearing this sometimes made me feel a bit sad, as someone who wasn't a monk but who had visited the temple many times. One day, the priest explained what he meant:

*"I have no disciples. This is because no one follows the path of Nen Buddhism by my own arrangement. It is only through the working of the Buddha that anyone walks this path. If I called someone my disciple, it would go against this principle. Besides, deciding who is a disciple or who 'belongs' easily leads to rivalries and divisions. People come together when there is a natural connection, and they part ways when that connection fades. That's simply how relationships work."*

In reality, many people admired the priest and visited the temple regularly. But his point was that Nen Buddhism is about recognizing our inability to become Buddha on our own, and about listening, together, to the Buddha's voice. Because Buddha's working is both personal and universal, there is no need for hierarchies like teacher and disciple, leader and follower.

In Theravada Buddhism, those who achieve awakening by hearing the Buddha's teachings are called voice hearers. For the priest, if there were any disciples at all, they would be disciples of the Buddha—the original voice they were all trying to hear—not his own.

The priest's words carried a subtle warning: the moment we define roles like "master" and "disciple" or start deciding who is "in" and who is "out," we begin to lose the free, dynamic flow that nourishes our awakening. Relationships become fixed, and creativity and openness are diminished. Real connection, the priest suggested, thrives in a flexible, open atmosphere where the Buddha's voice can be heard and shared by all, without barriers.

## No Self, No Buddha

The temple priest sometimes said things that seemed strikingly dismissive:

> "I simply trust Hōnen's teaching of Nen Buddhism, which says, 'Just call upon Amida Buddha, and through the Buddha's working, we are born in the Pure Land.' That's all there is for me. Whether Nen Buddhism truly leads us there, I do not know. Even if it turned out I was mistaken, or had been misled by Hōnen, I would not regret it.

*"If I could have become Buddha through some other practice and failed because I relied only on Nen, then maybe I would feel regret. But for someone like me, who can't follow any other path fully, there are no other options."*

He followed the path of Nen Buddhism with unwavering simplicity, showing the straightforward resolve of a being with human nature—someone who had given up trying to appear wise.

*"If the Primal Vow of Amida Buddha is true, then Gautama Buddha's teachings must also be true. If Gautama Buddha's teachings are true, then Hōnen's explanation of Nen Buddhism must also be true.*

*"If Hōnen's words are true, then my own voice, even if small and weak, cannot be meaningless. In short, my confidence as a fool stands on this ground. Whether you follow Nen Buddhism or turn away from it is entirely your choice."*

Over time, I realized that, for the priest, Nen Buddhism had thinned the usual sense of time to its bare minimum. By wholeheartedly surrendering himself to this single act of calling Amida's name, he dissolved even the notion of a timeline—from birth in the Pure Land to eventual Buddhahood—into nothing more than a simple thought of all-too-human being.

Furthermore, even the idea of an "I" who becomes Buddha had almost disappeared for him.

*"When you look deeply into the Primal Vow, the vow Amida Buddha formed over an immeasurable span of time, you find it exists solely for me."*

At first glance, saying that Amida Buddha exists only for oneself might seem self-centered. But once you fully realize the impossibility of helping yourself through your own will, you see that this present self, here and now, is the only point where acceptance can occur. In the vastness of the Long Now, the present moment narrows to a single point, from which a clear calling emerges. Without "I," there is no Buddha. Buddha needs a meeting point to emerge, and the meeting point is exactly where I am.

## The Voice Heard

To let go of trying to appear wise is to step away from words themselves. We rely so heavily on words to think, but this approach encourages us to go beyond that. In Nen Buddhism, this path leads us past the meanings of "*Naam Aami Daab*" as mere written words, guiding us toward pure sound, pure voice.

Long ago, even before Hōnen, there was a Nen Buddhist follower named Kyōshin. He was not a monk. He lived apart from everyday society, dedicating himself to calling, stripping away words until only a single, pure voice remained.

In his later years, the mountain temple priest embodied this attitude. Free from personal intention, he accepted everything as it was, moving naturally with the stream of life.

> *"Buddha's essence is beyond my understanding. It has no form, no color, and cannot be expressed by words or captured by thought."*

In his final days, he seemed to let go of everything, embracing each moment as it was. Even his practices of calling and mindful listening became almost imperceptible, leaving only the voice—the simple presence of sound arising and being heard. It was living without clinging to meaning or goals. It reminds me of the Zen monk Ryōkan's teaching: "When it's time to die, just die."

In that view, distinctions such as good and bad, human and Buddha, dissolved. By moving beyond these divisions, he could hear the voice of becoming

Buddha, and the priest floated gently in a realm of non-duality.

I wonder if I, too, might live that way someday. But perhaps that "someday" is already beginning— in small, imperfect ways.

In Japan, there is a quiet tradition of seeing work not as a transaction but as a form of practice—a way to polish the self through daily tasks, routines, and shared responsibilities. Monks clean not just to tidy the space but to sweep the mind. In that same spirit, perhaps our workplaces, too, can be viewed not as battlefields for competition but as dojos—training grounds for presence, patience, and compassion.

To work like a monk, then, is to treat one's work not as a means to an end, but as a mirror—one that reflects who we are becoming, shaped day by day by our habits and habitats. I am not yet there. But for now, I will keep practicing—wholeheartedly embracing what is, and quietly aligning myself with what might be.

That is my way of walking, and working, like a monk.

# Afterword

Recently, during an important online meeting, I glanced out the window and noticed one of our cats staring at me—but this cat was supposed to be safely indoors. Realizing it had escaped, I momentarily lost my composure, visibly surprising the participants. My first response was frustration, but then I remembered the teachings of Nen Buddhism, and something shifted.

The cat, after all, was calm. I was the one panicking. I smiled inwardly: "Here I am again, being very human." My irritation melted away.

These small moments—unexpected, imperfect, emotional—are where Buddhist wisdom meets daily life.

In this afterword, I reflect on how Buddhist teachings can guide us—not as distant ideals, but as tools for navigating the challenges of work, society, and being human.

We are living in times of confusion and uncertainty: rapid technological advancement, the lingering impact of the pandemic, global environmental crises, and the resurgence of war and conflict. Amid all of this, what wisdom can Buddhism, a tradition carried forward for more than twenty-five hundred years, offer us today?

This is precisely the question explored in the dialogue between the businessperson and the monk presented in this book. Each figure represents an aspect of my own identity: the businessperson reflects the logic and mindset of contemporary society, while the priest's words draw from the wisdom of several exceptional Buddhist figures, from Gautama Buddha to historical teachers such as Hōnen and Shinran, as well as contemporary monks I've met in person. While the story draws heavily from my own perspective and experience, some elements—such as the businessperson's illness—are not autobiographical. They reflect the uncertainty and suffering we all face in life, inspired by the experiences of close friends and family. If my book has offered even a spark of insight or inspiration in your everyday life, I would be truly delighted.

During the last two decades, I have been dedicated to bridging the gap between Buddhist wisdom and modern society. My initial efforts were aimed at teaching business frameworks to Buddhist temple priests responsible for temple management. While serving as a Buddhist monk, I pursued an MBA outside Japan to gain a deeper understanding of modern economic systems, hoping to connect these two seemingly distant worlds.

One of my initial surprises during my MBA classes was the casual and frequent use of terminology derived from warfare, such as *strategy*. Indeed, business schools themselves seemed like military academies for the business world, always promoting methods to defeat competitors. Immersed in this environment, I gradually started to feel uneasy. I couldn't help but wonder, *Could the persistence of war metaphors in business—given its outsized influence—be subtly reinforcing patterns of competition and division, even beyond the workplace?* After all, when we constantly speak of "targets, defeating rivals, or capturing market share," we may unconsciously reinforce a worldview grounded in zero-sum thinking. This mindset can easily bleed into politics, international relations, and even personal behavior and undermine the habits of listening, empathy, and coexistence that peace requires. In contrast, Buddhism pursues not *victory* but *mastery*—a profound understanding and transcending of oneself. It struck me that this shift could hold a vital clue for the future of the business world.

Upon returning to Japan, I founded the Temple Management School to explore how Buddhist wisdom—particularly the shift from *victory* to *mastery*—might offer new models of leadership and organizational culture. I began by sharing these insights with more than eight hundred Buddhist priests.

Over time, this initiative naturally expanded beyond the temple walls. Leaders from the corporate world began reaching out, seeking ways to integrate Buddhist principles into management. One notable example involved a law firm in Washington, DC, requesting a resident "monk manager" to bring hope and healing to an overwhelmed workplace.

Through these experiences, I began assuming the role of a "futurist monk." My one-on-one dialogues with executives frequently go beyond immediate problem-solving to explore fundamental existential questions such as "Why does this company exist?" and "What truly constitutes happiness?" Indeed, the questions of suffering and happiness, which have been explored in Buddhism for millennia, are just as relevant to modern organizations.

As these conversations deepened, they led me to an even more profound inquiry: "What can we leave behind for future generations?"

Translating Roman Krznaric's *The Good Ancestor* into Japanese spurred me to raise this question worldwide. This inquiry has resonated deeply with many leaders, who have expressed a desire to "leave future generations with more choices."

However, contemplating our legacy inevitably confronts us with a profound sense of disconnection prevalent in modern society. Many today feel isolated—not only from others, but also from the environment and from meaningful continuity with future generations. Without a clear sense of connection, the future can appear daunting and uncertain.

One response to this sense of disconnection is the Camphor Tree Village Project at Musashino University, which explores how we might reposition ourselves within a broader web of life—connecting with the environment, other beings, and future generations through intergenerational living and ecological reflection.

But how can we practically embody these profound insights in our everyday lives?

I believe People's Buddhism, particularly Nen Buddhism, offers valuable wisdom. Nen Buddhism does not idealize human nature; instead, it starts by deeply acknowledging our weaknesses and limitations.

For example, in our daily lives at work or at home, we often experience moments of irritation or anger. By applying mindful listening, as taught in Nen Buddhism, we can calmly accept our emotions and those of others, transforming conflicts into mutual understanding. Embracing our mistakes and openly admitting, "I am human," allows us to move forward even in challenging circumstances.

A more grounded life begins when we fully recognize and accept where we currently stand. Growth becomes possible the moment we courageously embrace our imperfections. Rooted in this view, People's Buddhism gives us the gentle strength to keep walking—especially when we lose our way.

Whoever you are, I believe this timeless wisdom can help you recalibrate your direction, just as the Buddha serves not as a goal to be achieved, but as a guiding north star by which we navigate.

May this book be something you return to—not to find answers, but to remember your direction. A quiet encounter with a temple priest. A pause in the day. A way to listen again.

That, too, is how we work like a monk.

# Acknowledgments

This book emerged through years of dialogue—
between past and present, tradition and modernity, self and society. I would like to express my
deepest gratitude to those who helped shape it.

First and foremost, I am indebted to Rev. Shinsho
Kajita and the community at Hōnen-in, Kyoto, whose
presence helped inspire the character of the temple
priest. Likewise, I am grateful to Rev. Wakei Iwagami
and the sangha at Komyoji Temple in Kamiyacho,
Tokyo, who helped bring the voice of the businessperson into clearer focus.

I also bow in reverence to the many Buddhist
teachers across time—from Shakyamuni Buddha,
Nāgārjuna, Hōnen, and Shinran to countless others,
whose words and insights form the deep current
flowing through this story.

To my dear colleagues at the Institute for Temple Management (Mirai no Jushoku-Juku)—Kaori

Matsuzaki, Takuya Endo, Tomohiro Kimura, and the many Buddhist priests I've met through the school and our podcasts—thank you for shaping this "People's Buddhism" through shared experimentation and care.

Special thanks to my team at Interbeing Inc.— Hiroko Onari and Kenji Yoshihira and to Eriko Tsumori and Kumiko Seto for their invaluable editorial collaboration and heartfelt encouragement throughout this journey.

I especially wish to acknowledge the companions who walked beside me during the Camphor Tree Village Project at Musashino University: Teruma Nishimoto, Chikou Iwagami, Ruriko Watanabe, Kenta Suzuki, Toshihiro Omi, Junichi Kato, Jun Hirata, Yu Koseki, and many other colleagues and students whose presence enriched the project in quiet yet meaningful ways.

I am also thankful to Ashi Kesang Choden Wangchuck, Lady Mariéme Jamme, Ephraim Jose, Roman Krznaric, David Atkinson, Stephen Batchelor, Pico Iyer, Yutaka Morishima, David Rodin, David Kennedy, Izumi Nakamitsu, Markus Gabriel, and Yuval Noah Harari, whose in-person dialogues inspired new dimensions in this work. Our conversations helped me deepen my understanding of the intersections between Buddhism, ecology, and intergenerational ethics.

This project could not have taken shape without the early belief and support of Uni Agency, especially Michiko Urata and Takeshi Oyama. I am also deeply grateful to the team at Simon & Schuster UK, whose trust, clarity, and editorial insight guided the English edition from the very beginning. To all my publishers and literary agents across the globe, thank you for believing in the vision of reimagining Buddhist wisdom for a wider audience.

This book is an experiment in translation—not just between languages, but between traditions, generations, and ways of life. Some expressions intentionally depart from doctrinal precision to create interpretive bridges: simple, accessible entry points for those unfamiliar with Pure Land teachings.

To fellow monastics and Dharma companions, thank you for embracing this experiment with warmth and patience. I hope it will encourage wider appreciation of our tradition and gently open new doors for curious readers. And to Ana Ilievska—along with many other friends whose names are too many to list—thank you for your thoughtful proofreading and intellectual companionship. I hope this experiment contributes, in some small way, to a broader and more inclusive conversation—within Buddhist communities and beyond.

Finally, I wish to thank my family and intimate friends—from distant island shores to close

neighborhood corners—whose quiet encouragement, laughter, and presence have sustained me
more than words can say. Your support has helped
me keep walking—with presence, with care, and
with the resolve to work like a monk.

# About the Author

**Shoukei Matsumoto** is a Buddhist monk and philosopher who bridges ancient spiritual wisdom with the urgent challenges of the twenty-first century. He is the author of the global bestseller *A Monk's Guide to a Clean House and Mind* and *A Quiet Mind*. Drawing on his deep spiritual practice, Shoukei collaborates with world-leading intellectuals and business leaders, offering a Buddhist-informed yet radically practical vision of leadership, well-being, and collective responsibility. His unique approach to People's Buddhism has facilitated work with many renowned world-class institutions, including the United Nations and the World Economic Forum.